LARGER

★ *THAN* ★

LIFE

LYNDON B. JOHNSON
and the
RIGHT TO VOTE

LARGER

★ *THAN* ★

LIFE

ANNE QUIRK

Norton Young Readers
An Imprint of W. W. Norton & Company
Independent Publishers Since 1923

For information about permission to reproduce selections from this book, write to
Permissions, W. W. Norton & Company, Inc., 500 Fifth Avenue, New York, NY 10110

For information about special discounts for bulk purchases, please contact
W. W. Norton Special Sales at specialsales@wwnorton.com or 800-233-4830

Manufacturing by Lake Book Manufacturing
Book design by Beth Steidle
Production manager: Julia Druskin

Library of Congress Cataloging-in-Publication Data
Names: Quirk, Anne, author.
Title: Larger than life : Lyndon B. Johnson and the right to vote / Anne Quirk.
Other titles: Lyndon B. Johnson and the right to vote
Description: First edition. | New York, NY: Norton Young Readers, 2021. |
Includes bibliographical references and index. | Audience: Ages 9–12
Identifiers: LCCN 2021019762 | ISBN 9781324015543 (hardcover) |
ISBN 9781324015550 (epub)
Subjects: LCSH: Johnson, Lyndon B. (Lyndon Baines), 1908–1973—Juvenile
literature. | United States. Voting Rights Act of 1965—Juvenile literature. | African
Americans—Suffrage—History—20th century—Juvenile literature. | Suffrage—United
States—History—20th century—Juvenile literature. | Civil rights movements—United
States—History—20th century—Juvenile literature. | Presidents—United States—
Biography—Juvenile literature. | United States—Politics and government—
1963–1969—Juvenile literature.
Classification: LCC E847 .Q57 2021 | DDC 973.923092 [B]—dc23
LC record available at https://lccn.loc.gov/2021019762

W. W. Norton & Company, Inc., 500 Fifth Avenue, New York, N.Y. 10110
www.wwnorton.com

W. W. Norton & Company Ltd., 15 Carlisle Street, London W1D 3BS

2 4 6 8 9 0 7 5 3 1

For John R. Grant, fellow traveler

★ CONTENTS ★

LARGER

★ *THAN* ★

LIFE

IT IS WRONG—DEADLY WRONG—TO DENY ANY OF YOUR FELLOW AMERICANS THE RIGHT TO VOTE IN THIS COUNTRY.

—PRESIDENT LYNDON JOHNSON, MARCH 15, 1965

CHAPTER ONE

★ ★ ★

WASHINGTON, DC, MARCH 15, 1965

On Sunday, March 7, 1965, hundreds of Americans were beaten, bloodied, and gassed by state troopers and local police officers when they tried to march across the Edmund Pettus Bridge in Selma, Alabama.

Eight days later, on March 15, President Lyndon Baines Johnson, who didn't like giving speeches and wasn't very good at it, delivered the best speech of his life. He stood at a podium in the well of the House Chamber, the great hall in the United States Capitol Building where the House of Representatives meets.

Just behind Johnson, in a matched pair of oversized chairs, sat Hubert Humphrey, the vice president of the United States—whose official duties include presiding over the Senate—and John McCormack, the Massachusetts congressman who served as Speaker of the House. The vice

President Lyndon B. Johnson addresses a joint session of Congress on the right to vote, March 15, 1965.

president was straight-backed and alert. The seventy-three-year-old Speaker was equally engaged, but frail, sometimes looking as though he might slide off his imposing seat.

Almost every member of the House of Representatives was in the chamber that night. So were nearly every senator, all nine Supreme Court justices, and each member of the president's cabinet. The longtime head of the Federal Bureau of Investigation, J. Edgar Hoover, was there. Mrs. Johnson was side by side with her oldest daughter, Lynda. There were no empty seats in the hall. There wasn't much more standing room in its aisles, either. Tens of millions of Americans watched the speech on their televisions. Those with the most up-to-date equipment were even able to view it in color.

But all five representatives from Mississippi and both of its senators—the state's entire congressional delegation—boycotted the event. They knew what was coming, and they wanted no part of it.

"I speak tonight," began the president, "for the dignity of man and the destiny of democracy."

His voice was steady, but his eyelids drooped, as though he hadn't slept well for days, or maybe weeks. Perhaps even years.

More than a century had passed since slavery was abolished, he reminded his audience. Nearly that long had elapsed since African American citizens had been assured the right to vote. Yet, throughout a vast region of the country, Black Americans were being systemically denied their civil rights—their legal privileges as citizens—by state and local laws that were cruel, hateful, and wrong.

No one in the chamber that night—or in homes across the country—could possibly have forgotten the atrocities that had just occurred in Selma, Alabama, but Johnson still recounted the attack on "long-suffering men and women [who] peacefully protested the denial of their rights as Americans. Many were brutally assaulted. One good man, a man of God, was killed."

Our consciences, the president insisted, and our Constitution demand action. Right here, right now.

He promised that in two days, he would send a detailed proposal—a bill—to Congress for a national voting rights law

Vice President Hubert
Humphrey (left), who also
serves as president of the
Senate, and Speaker of the
House John McCormack (right)
sit behind the president.

that would secure the most basic right of a democratic nation: the right to vote.

Our nation has been blighted for too long by bigotry and injustice, he insisted. We can't wait any longer to solve these problems. They will not be easy to overcome, he admitted, but they must be overcome.

"And we shall overcome."

A jolt passed through the great hall and the nation.

Lyndon Johnson was reciting the pledge of civil rights activists. This white man with deep roots in the South—this lifelong politician with a history of accommodating segregationists and compromising with white supremacists—was adding his voice to the chorus of men and women who had taken to the streets, marching, singing, sometimes even risking their lives, for racial justice.

The president of the United States was declaring that the nation would finally fulfill its promise that all Americans were created equal, not just some Americans.

"And we shall overcome."

A few congressmen sat on their hands, kept their faces blank, fixed their eyes on the middle distance, but most of the chamber erupted in cheers. Up in the gallery, where the visitors sat, tears flowed.

Martin Luther King Jr., the most prominent civil rights leader of his time, watched the speech from a friend's home in Alabama. The thirty-six-year-old was world famous, the most recent recipient of the Nobel Peace Prize. He was polished, thoughtful, and dignified. He was not a crier.

But that night, Martin Luther King Jr. cried.

The president wasn't ready to sit down—not yet. He spoke about a job he had in 1928, at a school in a town in south Texas. Back then, he was twenty years old, taking a year off from Southwest Texas State Teachers College because he couldn't afford its twenty-dollar-per-semester tuition.

Like most gifted storytellers—and canny politicians—LBJ

was more than willing to stray from the facts when it served his purpose. The tale he told that night wasn't accurate in every detail, but it was true in the deepest way: it came from his heart.

"My first job after college was as a teacher in Cotulla, Texas, in a small Mexican-American school," he recalled, even though he was actually still in college at the time. Johnson's lack of a diploma was one of the reasons he got the job in the first place. An experienced teacher would have cost more and might also have refused to work with non-Anglo students.

"Few of them could speak English," he explained about the pupils at the Welhausen School, "and I couldn't speak much Spanish. My students were poor and they often came to class without breakfast, hungry. They knew, even in their youth, the pain of prejudice. They never seemed to know why people disliked them. But they knew it was so, because I saw it in their eyes," he said. "Somehow you never forget what poverty and hatred can do when you see its scars on the hopeful face of a young child.

"I never thought then, in 1928, that I would be standing here in 1965," he said, taking another short detour from the facts. Even as a twenty-year-old, perhaps even as a ten-year-old, Lyndon Johnson had set his sights on getting to the White House eventually.

"It never even occurred to me in my fondest dreams that I might have the chance to help the sons and daughters of those students, and to help people like them all over this country."

Then he leaned over the podium, extending each imposing inch of his six-foot three-inch frame. "But now I do have that chance—and I'll let you in on a secret," he said, a sly smile playing across his face.

"I mean to use it."

DIDN'T MATTER WHERE HE WAS, HE WAS ALWAYS RUNNING, RUNNING, RUNNING.

— JESSIE JOHNSON HATCHER, REMEMBERING HER NEPHEW'S CHILDHOOD

CHAPTER TWO

★ ★ ★

STONEWALL, TEXAS, AUGUST 27, 1908

At daybreak on August 27, 1908, in a two-room house outside the tiny village of Stonewall, Texas, a baby boy was born to Rebekah and Sam Johnson. The new parents boasted that their first child weighed a whopping eleven pounds at birth, but their estimate was likely on the generous side. Few farmhouses came equipped with reliable baby scales in the early twentieth century—or now, for that matter— and the newborn's mother and father were bred-in-the-bone Texans, proud descendants of settlers who came to the region in the 1850s. Beneath the endless sky of the Lone Star State, there was plenty of room for ranches or fortunes or dreams to grow. Everything was larger there, maybe even babies.

Yet there was no denying that the new Johnson baby was *big*. He had the darkest brown eyes, a prominent nose, and

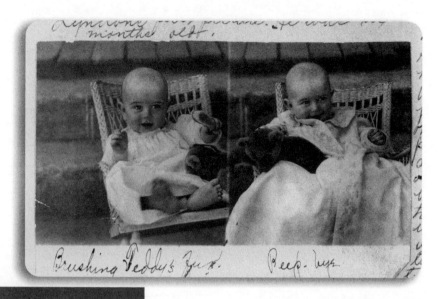

Six-month-old Lyndon with his teddy bear, 1909.

tremendous ears, just like his father. All he lacked, at least for his first several months, was a first name.

Rebekah Baines Johnson was a college graduate, a rare accomplishment in those days for women—and men, too—in the isolated towns in the Hill Country of central Texas. Sam Johnson was a farmer, for the time being, but he had served in the Texas state legislature and saw himself returning to public life eventually.

Both of the baby's parents loved politics. Long before they were attracted to each other, they were drawn to public affairs. (A speech by William Jennings Bryan, the golden-tongued Nebraska Democrat who made three unsuccessful runs for the presidency, was the setting for an early date.) The young couple believed that government, when it was run properly and fairly, could improve the everyday lives of ordinary Americans.

Many of their neighbors in Stonewall struggled to feed their families. None of them was looking for a handout, but when hard times came around—and hard times always came back around eventually, especially in Texas—some people just needed a little more help, that's all.

The Johnsons were convinced that better roads, built by the state with tax dollars, and public schools, paid for by local citizens, would bring more jobs and real prosperity to the small towns of the Hill Country.

The Johnsons were full of high hopes for themselves, for the people of the Hill Country, and of course for their brand new baby. No ordinary name would do for their sure-to-be-extraordinary child.

For three months, Rebekah and Sam pondered hundreds of names for their firstborn, before rejecting all of them. Finally, Sam proposed Linden, the last name of an attorney he admired. It sounded good to Rebekah, more or less, but she couldn't help herself from making some adjustments. So, after tinkering a little with spelling and pronunciation, their son became Lyndon Baines Johnson.

The last name came from his father's side, the middle name from his mother's, but the first name was all his own.

Little Lyndon could still fit in his father's arms when he debuted at Stonewall's annual spring picnic, one of the town's most popular events. Sam Johnson was tall and friendly, an outgoing, backslapping sort of a man who knew how to charm his past (and likely future) constituents in the Hill Country. But despite his skills as a crowd pleaser, the thirty-one-year-old

At a year and a half, 1910.

proved no match for his infant child. All the baby had to do was turn on his bright smile and waggle his pudgy arms, and the picnickers fell in love.

"You've got a politician there," Eddie Hahn, a friend of the family, informed Sam. "He's a chip off the old block. I can see him running for office twenty years from now."

(Mr. Hahn's political predictions turned out to be off by a few years, although he clearly had a sharp eye for talent. Lyndon would be eight years past his twentieth birthday when he made his first run for office.)

Once Rebekah Johnson's boy got the hang of walking, he took to wandering, a tendency that terrified his young mother.

A small-town Texas boy in cowboy hat and overalls, around 1915.

The Pedernales River flowed just a few hundred yards away from the family home, and it attracted its share of poisonous snakes. A child could all too easily be bitten by the serpents or slip and drown in the stream's murky waters. Rebekah feared for the safety of her roving tot—any parent would—but there were always more chores to do and there was often a new baby wailing for her attention. She just couldn't get her oldest to stay put. Nobody could.

The Junction School, about a mile down the road, was Lyndon's favorite destination. Its one room and one teenaged teacher served around thirty-five students who spanned eight full grades. The sociable Johnson boy was drawn to the sounds of children playing in its schoolyard, and he adored their instructor, Miss Kate. Every chance he could, the four-year-old climbed onto her lap. Whenever she sat down, he clambered back up to his old spot.

Fierce wails and bone-rattling howls broke out whenever Lyndon's parents tried to pry their son away from Miss Kate's classroom. Eventually, the Johnsons surrendered to the inevitable. The overstretched schoolmistress found a way to squeeze one more child into the building.

In his first days as an official student, Lyndon strolled hand in hand to the Junction School with his mother. Before too long, he arrived on the back of his cousin Ava's donkey. At first, he sat behind Ava. Then he sat in front of Ava. Then he got his own donkey.

In 1913, when Lyndon was five, the family moved to Johnson City, thirteen miles away from Stonewall. It wasn't much of a city, just a few hundred residents, but its school boasted several classrooms, not just one, and there was a hotel, a bank, and a courthouse. Best of all, it was *Johnson* City, founded by an ancestor. Lyndon's father had grown up in Johnson City. Lyndon's grandfather and great uncle, who were in the cattle business, had once been its most prominent citizens.

In Johnson City, it meant something to be a Johnson.

The family's new home was near the center of town and was one of its nicest residences. A pair of side porches gave Sam the space he required for long chats with neighbors. Six rooms inside the house, and a sleeping porch out back, quickly filled up with Johnsons. Little sisters Rebekah and Josepha arrived

The family home in Johnson City, Texas.

before the move into town; brother Sam arrived afterward, in 1914, followed two years later by the family's baby, Lucia.

Although Rebekah Johnson dearly loved her five children, she took little pleasure in ironing their clothes, or tidying up their rooms, or preparing their meals. Reading was far more to her taste than sweeping. Drearier household chores fell to hired help, when the family could afford it, or her mother, Grandma Baines, when they couldn't. Determined to put her college education to use, Mrs. Johnson wrote for Johnson City's weekly newspaper, contributed to publications in Austin and Dallas, and founded a local literary society for her fellow bookworms. She also gave elocution lessons and taught poetry, turning one of those side porches into an outdoor classroom when the weather allowed. Upon observing that the town's

Lyndon in 1921 with his three sisters, Lucia, Josepha, and Rebekah (left to right), and his brother, Sam.

teenagers were sorely lacking in social graces, she became a dance instructor, hoping that waltzing might smooth away some of the rougher edges of adolescence.

Sam Johnson dabbled in a variety of occupations. He bought and sold property. He owned a movie house for a while and acquired a newspaper for his wife to edit. But the only job he really loved—and the only one at which he excelled—was politics. In 1917, after ten years as a private citizen, he ran for election and won his old seat in the Texas legislature.

During his first stint in the legislature, in the years before his marriage, Sam Johnson had helped to preserve the Alamo, the old Spanish mission church in San Antonio that symbolized

Lone Star grit. When he returned to the Texas House of Representatives a decade later, Sam convinced the state to invest in the paved roads that the Hill Country desperately needed. He persuaded his fellow legislators to provide assistance—seeds for new crops and feed for hungry livestock—to the west Texas farmers devastated by the droughts of 1919 and 1920. At a time when the majority of his legislative colleagues kept quiet about the horrors of the Ku Klux Klan, Sam Johnson spoke out forcefully against the homegrown hooded terrorists who were murdering Black people throughout Texas, and tormenting Jews and Catholics, too. His courage earned him death threats, which he took pride in ignoring.

As often as he could, Lyndon jumped in the family's Model T Ford and accompanied his father to Austin, bumping along the unpaved roads that Sam Johnson was trying to improve. Designed to impress—wrapped in red granite, topped by a great dome, rising from one of the hilly city's most prominent mounds—the Texas State Capitol building was the biggest structure the young Johnson boy had ever seen, or would see for many years to come. (Not even the United States Capitol, which Lyndon Johnson would come to dominate in another thirty years, was as large as its Texas counterpart.) Prowling around such a place was thrilling for Lyndon, even when he barely grasped the point of all its offices and meeting rooms, or the purpose of all those people who rushed in and out of them.

Back at home in Johnson City, cozying up to his chatty father, the attentive son received his real education in Texas politics. Nothing pleased Sam Johnson more than telling tales about his colorful colleagues in Austin, and his firstborn never tired of hearing them.

"Sitting there in the half-light of dawn, my feet not quite touching the floor, I would listen for hours," Lyndon recalled years later. "Naturally, I couldn't really understand most of what he told me, but I could sense it was all very important and sometimes very funny."

In 1918, Texas governor William Pettus Hobby came to the Johnson home for dinner. It was supposed to be an adults-only meal, but ten-year-old Lyndon found a way to tuck himself under the dining room table—keeping his long legs from bumping up against the grown-ups—and stay hidden for the entire meal. It must have been an agonizing evening for the restless boy, but the pain was worth it. Governors didn't come by every day.

Around the same time, Lyndon set up a shoeshine stand at the town's barbershop. He didn't do it for the money, although he was happy to have some extra coins in his pocket. He did it for the eavesdropping. Something about taking a seat in a barber's chair transformed even the quietest man into an avid talker. In Johnson City, as in many small towns around America, all the best local gossip circulated first inside the barbershop.

Young Lyndon wasn't missing a word of it.

But as he grew older and his family's life got harder, the talk inside the barbershop, and all around Johnson City, became more difficult for him to hear.

Sam Johnson was a failure. That's what people were saying. Aside from politics—and no one could feed a family on the puny salary that part-time legislators earned—Lyndon's father couldn't do anything right. He paid too much for the buildings, and then sold them for too little. He borrowed heavily to acquire more land and more farming equipment. When the droughts came, his crops were ruined, making it impossible for him to repay his loans. Before too long, he owed almost everyone in town, with little hope of paying any of them back.

Lyndon's father wasn't a lazy man. He had always been a hard worker.

It's possible that bad luck was the source of Sam's troubles. Maybe, as Lyndon's uncle Tom Johnson figured, Sam was cursed. "If you want a business to be jinxed," he sighed, "go into it with Sam."

But it's more likely that Sam Johnson's real obstacle was less colorful than a hex and much tougher to overcome. Maybe Lyndon's father was just born in the wrong place, at the wrong time. The Hill Country that he loved so deeply was a hard place to make a living in the early twentieth century; it was too poor for any of Sam's big dreams to come true.

Few people in Johnson City had extra money to spend on movies or hotels or newspapers. They struggled to feed themselves and their families. They made do without electricity, without indoor plumbing, without more than a few years of schooling. The beautiful land they owned came with a cruel streak. You couldn't count on a cotton or wheat crop to come in each year. You couldn't count on cattle to survive a scorching summer. No matter how hard you worked, or how much you sacrificed, in the Hill Country, you just couldn't count on your life working out the way you hoped.

By the early 1920s, Lyndon's family had tumbled from the top of the heap in Johnson City to a spot far closer to the bottom. Although the Johnsons always had a roof over their heads and food on their table, the children's meals got skimpier and their clothes shabbier. Meaner gossips around town took pleasure in noting that Rebekah's fancy college degree and refined manners weren't doing her much good anymore. Stories circulated about Sam's drinking problem.

Lyndon hated his family's drop in status. He despised being just another of the many poor kids in town. He started slacking off at school, staying out late, mouthing off to his parents. After finishing the eleventh grade, the highest year of education at Johnson City High School, he refused to go on to college.

Rebekah Johnson, who took such pride in her own education, was furious. She warned Lyndon that he was throwing away his chance at making something of himself. For the first time in their lives—the only time in their lives— mother and son fought each other tooth and nail.

Yet Mrs. Johnson held on to the hope that Lyndon would someday shake off his teenaged obstinacy and become a great man. She had always been convinced that her children were special, a cut above the others around town. "Some children are born to follow," she often said, although it's unlikely her neighbors appreciated this opinion of hers. "My children were born to lead."

Grandmother Baines, a regular visitor to the Johnson home, held her own opinion about Lyndon's future.

"That boy," the plainspoken widow said confidently, "is going to wind up in the penitentiary—just mark my words."

I WAS DETERMINED TO GIVE THEM
WHAT THEY NEEDED TO MAKE IT IN THIS
WORLD, TO HELP THEM FINISH THEIR
EDUCATION. THEN THE REST WOULD
TAKE CARE OF ITSELF.

*—LYNDON JOHNSON ON HIS STUDENTS
IN COTULLA, TEXAS*

CHAPTER THREE

★ ★ ★

COTULLA, TEXAS, 1927

The Blanco County jail was a short stroll from LBJ's childhood home. Square and squat, the two-story structure was made out of light-colored limestone blocks that periodically gave way to iron-barred windows. Built long before Lyndon was born and still used for decades after his death, the jail was a constant reminder to the people of Johnson City, Texas, especially its young people, that crime (usually) didn't pay.

Lyndon got the message. To his grandmother's surprise and his mother's relief, the oldest Johnson child never spent a night in the local jail, or in the Texas State Penitentiary in Huntsville, or in any other sort of correctional institution in any other state.

But for most of the 1920s, throughout his teenage years, Lyndon was pretty much a mess.

Lyndon as an older teenager, perhaps around the time he enrolled at Southwest Texas State Teachers College in San Marcos.

Soon after high school graduation, he took a job on a road crew near Johnson City. Later, briefly, he was employed at an East Texas cotton gin— where cotton seeds are picked off the plant and the fiber is then crushed into bales. The work was hard and hot, and the cotton gin had the drawback of being deafening, too. Lyndon hated manual labor. He was too skinny, too weak, and probably too full of himself to be any good at it.

There must be, he figured, a better way to earn a living.

When he heard that some older friends were heading

west to California, Lyndon packed his bag, sneaked out of his family's home, and hopped aboard a beat-up old Ford. His parents were up in arms when they discovered what their stubborn son had done, but they couldn't force him to come back home—not if he was determined to get out of Texas. Back then, before air travel was easy and interstate highways were common, the West Coast was a lot farther away from Johnson City than it is now. Telephones were rare in rural areas in 1924; cell phones and internet connections were the stuff of science fiction.

Sixteen-year-old Lyndon was on his own when he jumped into his friends' jalopy, well beyond the reach of Sam and Rebekah Johnson.

In his later years, when he was famous and powerful, Johnson told stories about being an unknown and powerless young vagabond. He recalled sleeping under the stars because he couldn't afford a room, broiling under the fierce sun of the Golden State while laboring long days as a field hand, and fretting, on the darkest nights, about where he might find his next meal. Johnson spoke of homesickness so heavy that it nearly crushed him after two years away from the Hill Country. He described rolling up his meager possessions, sticking out his thumb, and hitchhiking back to the people he loved and the land he missed.

Most of this was poppycock.

The fact of the matter was this: the young Texan spent very little time as a farm laborer in California—maybe no time at all. Soon after arriving in the state, he was given an office job by his cousin, Tom Martin, a lawyer who lived in the fast-growing city of San Bernardino, about sixty miles east of Los Angeles. Attorney Martin's legal practice appeared to be flourishing, and he generously purchased two new suits for his lanky young relative and invited the teenager to live rent-free in his four-bedroom home.

The arrangement seemed ideal. Lyndon had no trouble imagining himself settling down in California, earning a law degree, and ripening into an attorney of importance and property, just like his cousin.

After a few months, though, the young Texan made a painful discovery. Lyndon's cousin turned out to be a heavy drinker and an unfaithful husband. When his wife went back to Texas for an extended family visit, Tom Martin moved his girlfriend into their home. An exuberant hostess, she threw open its doors—and liquor cabinet—and presided over an endless series of all-day and all-night parties, transforming a respectable residence into a boozy club house for San Bernardino's sketchier citizens. Attorney Martin neglected his legal duties and stopped paying his bills. Lyndon and the other young clerks at the firm, none of them members of the California bar, tried their best to keep the office running. They paid some the firm's expenses out of their own pockets, and they offered their own version of legal advice to clients.

That was a big mistake, as Lyndon soon realized.

In the state of California, as well as every other state, practicing law without a license is illegal. The young man from Johnson City might not have had a law degree, but he soon figured out that he could be charged with a crime. When Mrs. Martin returned to San Bernardino, driven there from Texas by her father-in-law, Lyndon talked his way into a ride back home. He didn't have to stick out his thumb or stand on the edges of lonely highways. He sat in the front seat of a late-model Buick.

Less than a year after running away in the middle of the night, Lyndon was back in his old house in Johnson City, and back on a road building crew, too. The work was brutally hard and soul-crushing—the scrawny teenager was sometimes yoked to an ox. Still, it was a paying job, the only one he could find. For a full year, he worked on the crew, probably hating each and every minute of it.

But the ordeal turned his life around, and it restored his faith in his mother. She was absolutely right: a college degree was a good thing to have.

The University of Texas was in nearby Austin, within easy walking distance of the state capitol building that Lyndon used to prowl around as a boy. Its sprawling campus was lined with handsome live oak trees. Its faculty was first-rate. Its football teams were nationally ranked. The most accomplished students in Texas, and surrounding states, were proud to call themselves Longhorns.

Very few of those young scholars, however, came from the Hill Country in the 1920s. UT's tuition was too high for their cash-strapped families, and its course work was too demanding academically. For Lyndon and most of his classmates, the state's best-known university was simply out of reach.

Those Johnson City High School graduates who sought to continue their education—and few did—usually went to Southwest Texas State Teachers College.

Commonly referred to as San Marcos, after its location in a small city about fifty miles southeast of Lyndon's hometown, the college charged a modest tuition of less than twenty dollars a semester, and its acceptance standards were lax. Even so, Lyndon barely squeaked in. Without some last-minute geometry tutoring from his mother, he probably would have flunked the required math exam.

In the spring of 1927, when he started at San Marcos, Lyndon was eighteen, about the same age as most of the other incoming students, but nearly three years had passed since he graduated from high school. Unless you considered staying out of a jail an accomplishment, he had very little to show for those years. College offered him a very welcome opportunity to start over.

And he was determined not to blow it.

Soon after arriving on campus, he wrangled a rent-free bed in a small apartment above the garage of the college's president, Dr. Cecil Evans. He also talked his way into a job with Dr. Evans.

Johnson wrote for the college newspaper, regularly contributing articles about his boss (and landlord). "Great as an educator and as an executive, Dr. Evans is greatest as a man," observed Lyndon. "He finds great happiness in serving others."

The shameless toadying worked. Dr. Evans took an immediate shine to his admirer from Johnson City.

So did several other professors on the receiving end of Johnson's fawning. The faculty at San Marcos, just like Miss Kate back at the Junction School in Stonewall, found Lyndon's single-minded devotion hard to resist.

"I've just met a boy who's going places," one professor gushed to another after his first encounter with Lyndon.

Students at San Marcos, on the other hand, held a lower opinion of their obsequious classmate. *Pedagog*, the college yearbook, illustrated Lyndon's name with a picture of a jackass. A humor column in the campus newspaper defined *bull* as the "Greek philosophy in which Lyndon Johnson has an M. B. degree." The *M* stood for "master's," and the *B* for an earthier way of saying "cow droppings."

Lyndon had few friends in college, and those he did have conceded that he could be hard to take. "He was never popular with his fellow students," recalled Willard Deason. "They thought he was arrogant." But Deason respected the doggedness that set Lyndon apart from his other classmates. "They may have been jealous of him because he had so much energy and could accomplish so much."

After a little more than a year in college, Lyndon was dead broke, mostly because he spent too much money on himself, especially on flashy clothes that flattered his hard-to-fit frame. The tuition at San Marcos might have been tiny, but he couldn't pay it, and neither could his parents. So, in the fall of 1928, just after his twentieth birthday, he took a teaching job in Cotulla, Texas, a small town between San Antonio and the Mexican border.

Johnson lacked a teaching degree, or any sort of teaching experience, but that wasn't a problem for his employer. The superintendent of schools in Cotulla wasn't looking for an experienced educator. He figured that no one with solid professional credentials would have even considered the job: the pay was awful and the students were Mexican American. Like all schools in Texas, and throughout the South, Cotulla schools were strictly segregated by race or ethnicity: Anglo kids went to school on the west side of town, Mexican Americans on the east.

Johnson didn't care which side of town the school was on. Just having a teaching job, or any sort of job, was good enough for him. A few years later, in the 1930s, when the United States fell into the Great Depression, steady employment became almost impossible to find in Texas—and almost everywhere else in the country. But rural America was suffering in the 1920s, too. Although big cities like New York and Chicago might have boomed during the decade known as the "Roaring Twenties," that prosperity seldom tricked down to small towns. For people who grew up in the Hill Country, a steady paycheck, even a minuscule one, was always prized.

For a salary of $125 a month, Lyndon was expected to be both a teacher and the principal of the Welhausen School. He didn't worry about being unqualified for either position. Or at least he didn't act worried.

Maybe he was just too busy.

Every skill that Lyndon possessed, he put to use at Welhausen. Nobody in the usually sleepy town of Cotulla had ever known anyone quite like Johnson. No other teacher or principal had ever worked as hard or as much as this skinny young man from Johnson City. Perhaps even more remarkably, he was doing all this for Mexican kids. Almost nobody in town had ever cared about *them* before.

The students at the school were flabbergasted by Johnson. The teachers were exhausted by him. Yet no one in Cotulla reacted to Lyndon the way his classmates did up in San Marcos. No one mocked him. No one thought he was full of himself. No one thought he was a big bag of wind, a bootlicker, or a bore.

In Cotulla, Lyndon Baines Johnson was loved.

Corporal punishment—a fancy way of saying "spanking"—was commonly used by teachers to discipline young students back in that era. Yet even the kids who were spanked by Johnson, and he spanked a lot of them, "still liked him," one student remembered. "He was the kind of teacher you wanted to work for."

When Lyndon was growing up, poverty was commonplace in and around Johnson City. He knew how it felt to worry about your next meal. But even so, the newcomer to south Texas was shocked by the hardships his Cotulla students endured. Almost all of them, for every single night of their childhood, went to bed hungry. Their houses were little more than shacks. Their clothes were rags. Their parents worked for pennies, when they worked at all.

It was hard to imagine a more hopeless place than the east side of Cotulla.

The Welhausen School
Athletic Club, with
Johnson in the last row—
Cotulla, Texas, 1928.

But Lyndon didn't give up. He couldn't. He had been raised to believe in hope and hard work and progress. He absolutely refused to lose faith in his students, any of them, or in himself. "I was determined," he said, remembering his students forty years later, "to spark something inside them, to fill their souls with ambition and interest and belief in the future."

Every child in America deserved an education. He was sure about this. Every family in America deserved a shot at success. He believed this, too.

Towering over his students and probably over almost everyone else in the town, Lyndon pushed himself into every aspect of his students' lives. He drilled them in English, force-fed them arithmetic, showered them with geography facts. He organized spelling bees and launched volleyball, track, and debating teams, making sure that each and every partic-ipant had rides for out-of-town competitions. He scratched a playground out of a dusty field and purchased bats and balls for the children to use in them. Any parent whose child missed school could expect a visit from the young principal, and then a torrent of verbal abuse if he didn't like their excuse for the absence.

Almost every morning, Lyndon was the first person to enter Welhausen. Almost every evening, he was the last person to depart.

He promised his students that each and every one of them could grow up to be the president of the United States. We're the greatest country on Earth, he told them, a land of limitless possibilities. He cautioned them, however, that they would have to wait their turn to move into the White House.

He was going to get there first.

I AM IN FAVOR OF GIVING BOTH THE WHITES AND THE BLACKS EQUAL RIGHTS, BUT NOT TOGETHER.

—SENATOR RICHARD RUSSELL

CHAPTER FOUR

★ ★ ★

WINDER, GEORGIA, MARCH 15, 1965

Senator Richard Russell wasn't in the great hall of the United States Capitol when President Johnson spoke out for civil rights. He wasn't even in Washington, DC. The sixty-seven-year-old was at his home in Winder, Georgia, on the evening of March 15, 1965, recovering from yet another flare-up of emphysema, the illness that was relentlessly destroying his lungs. It was a terrible ailment, eventually a fatal one, but the senator's respiratory difficulties didn't impair his thinking. His political reasoning was as sharp as ever.

As he listened to the president, Russell understood the historic importance of the address that Johnson—an old friend, political ally, and fellow member of the Democratic Party—was making to Congress and the American people.

And he must have been appalled by almost every word of it.

By the end of the Civil War, many of the South's largest cities, including Savannah (left; photographed in 1865) and Atlanta (1864), were in ruins.

No one, not even the president of the United States, needed to tell Richard Russell that the Civil War had been over for nearly a century. The Georgian was a loyal son of the Old South, well versed in his homeland's history, especially the blood-soaked years of 1861 to 1865. Though he wasn't born until 1897, more than thirty years after the Confederates surrendered to the Union Army, Russell had been raised to respect his forebears and honor their traditions.

He had been trained to carry on their grievances, too.

Before the Civil War, the Russells of Georgia owned gracious mansions and thriving businesses, made possible by the labor of enslaved people. After the Civil War, with slavery outlawed and the South in ruins, they lost nearly everything they possessed, except their pride.

Like most white voters in Georgia, and most white voters

throughout the states of the Old Confederacy, including LBJ's Texas, Richard Russell was a member of the Democratic Party. For nearly a hundred years, Southern Democrats blamed the party of Abraham Lincoln, the Republican Party, for the agonies of the Civil War and its aftermath. White Southerners were so reliably Democratic in those decades that they almost never voted for Republicans: not for mayor, not for governor, not for Congress, and not for president.

(Southern Black people, on the other hand—the few who could exercise their right to vote in the decades following the Civil War—strongly preferred Republicans.)

The way Senator Russell looked at it, the Civil War was never about slavery. It wasn't fought over whether one human being could claim to own another human being. To him, slavery was just the excuse that the Northern politicians used to seize Southern property and destroy Southern lives.

According to Senator Russell, the Civil War was a fight about power. It was a fight about democracy. It was a fight about whether the states in the South could make their own laws, live by their standards, follow their own traditions.

The Civil War was a fight about states' rights.

That struggle didn't end just because the South surrendered to the North in 1865. It simply took on a new shape.

Throughout his long political career, from his first days in the Georgia legislature until his final moments as a United States senator, Richard Russell was a tireless supporter of states' rights. Many other politicians shared his conviction that the federal government had seized too much power for itself, but few defended the principle of states' rights as eloquently, as frequently, and as fiercely as Russell did.

But states' rights represented more than just a political principle for the senator. It was also his rationalization for rejecting the founding ideals of the United States and for defying the Fifteenth Amendment to the United States Constitution, which plainly declared that no one could be denied the right to vote because of race or color.

Richard Russell was a white supremacist from the top of his balding head to the soles of well-shined shoes. He believed that white Americans were superior to Black Americans. "Any Southern white man worth a pinch of salt," he explained to friend in 1936, not long after he came north to Washington, "would give his all to maintain white superiority."

Senator Russell wholeheartedly supported racial segregation. He championed Jim Crow laws—an array of state and local laws in the South that strictly enforced separate schools for Black people, separate hospitals and separate sections on buses, in restaurants, and in movie theaters. These laws, Russell argued, promoted "the welfare and progress of both races." The wisdom of racial segregation, he explained, had been proven over time: "The whites and blacks alike in our section have learned that it is better for the races to live apart socially."

Other Southern politicians at the time, men like Theodore Bilbo from Mississippi or Cotton Ed Smith from South Carolina, tossed out racial slurs during congressional speeches or cheered on white thugs who preyed upon Black citizens.

Richard Russell was more dignified in his manner, more restrained in his speech. He maintained that he had nothing but respect for African Americans. "I was brought up with them," he insisted. "I love them."

Yet, when he served as governor of Georgia, from 1931 to 1933, Russell turned a blind eye as white Georgians lynched Black Georgians. He said nothing when white Georgians—displaying a lawless disregard for trials, judges, juries, or verdicts—accused Black Georgians of crimes, real or imagined, then strung them up on trees to die. He presided over a prison system that routinely employed torture, chains, and starvation to control its inmates, the majority of whom were Black.

Russell was a mere two months past his thirty-fifth birthday when he came to the Senate. Many of his colleagues in Congress were old enough to be his father. Some were nearly old enough to be his grandfather. But he won over his elders by memorizing all twenty-two of the Senate's formal rules and studying every page, all 1,326 of them, of the chamber's procedural guidelines. The diligent go-getter was soon rewarded with the Senate's greatest gifts: seats on its most powerful committees.

Even more generous were his fellow legislators from the South, a group known as the Southern bloc; these colleagues gave Russell their votes. With very few exceptions, whatever the senator from Georgia wanted from his fellow Southerners, the senator from Georgia received. On matters of major importance, few members of the bloc ever opposed their good friend from the Peachtree State.

From time to time during Russell's career in the Senate, Democrats from cooler climates would propose civil rights legislation—federal laws that would guarantee that all Black Americans, no matter where they lived, had the same rights as white Americans. The Southern bloc responded in the 1930s, 1940s, and 1950s by living up to its name: it blocked the bills.

Attempts to make lynching a federal crime, and to punish it in federal prisons, failed repeatedly because of the Southern bloc. Efforts to outlaw poll taxes—fees for voting, which primarily disadvantaged poor Southern Black people—went nowhere. During World War II, in the 1940s, the federal government did succeed in establishing an agency that was charged with ending racial discrimination in defense plants, but the Southern bloc made sure its administrators were routinely starved for cash.

After World War II, when President Harry Truman tried to desegregate the armed services—ending the practice of separating soldiers into Black and white units, finally allowing soldiers of all races to serve together—his proposed legislation was sidelined. Truman, a Missourian who had served in the Senate for more than a decade, got around his former colleagues by issuing a presidential order to integrate the military. But it was a half measure. Executive orders tend to be less enduring than laws passed by Congress; they are easier to overturn.

For decades, steadfast in his beliefs and supported by loyal allies, Richard Russell was able to kill, or severely hobble, every major civil rights bill that came before the Congress. It was an impressive record of legislative prowess.

It was also a shameful record.

And by the mid-1960s, it was being challenged as never before.

Born at the tail end of the nineteenth century, Russell had grown up in the era of horses and buggies and long memories, but cars were everywhere when he reached middle age, computers were coming online, and astronauts were being shot into space. The population of the nation was 125 million when Russell won his first senatorial campaign. By the 1960s, it was nearly 200 million.

The American people had become more ethnically and racially diverse, wealthier, healthier, and far better educated than earlier generations. They expected more from their political leaders. They expected more of themselves.

The fast-moving twentieth century transformed every region of the United States, even Russell's beloved South.

In what's now known as the Great Migration—a massive movement of African Americans that occurred over the course of fifty years—more than six million Black people left their homes in the rural South for densely populated cities in the North and West, places like Chicago, Detroit, Los Angeles, San Francisco, and New York. For the most part, these urban newcomers found steady work in their new homes, better housing for themselves, and better schools for their children. Many of these Black American citizens fought in World War II and the Korean War. They became taxpayers, and they became voters, too.

These former Southerners didn't believe that Jim Crow laws

had anything to do with states' rights. They knew full well that their constitutional rights had been violated back in Georgia or Mississippi because of their race. They knew that the rights of their families and friends who remained in the South were *still* being violated because of their race.

Russell waved off his critics. "We've had our problems," he said, speaking of his home region, "but we've solved them pretty well."

It's possible that some Americans, but probably only white Americans, believed Russell's sunny assurances of racial harmony in the South. But that untruth became harder and harder to believe in the 1950s and 1960s as a new generation of activists, especially a magnetic clergyman from Russell's own state, Martin Luther King Jr., became the leaders of the civil rights movement. More and more Americans, not just Black Americans, could see that something very wrong, something very dangerous, something deeply un-American had poisoned the hearts of powerful white Southerners like Richard Russell.

After enduring nearly a century of defeats in the United States Congress, civil rights advocates won a huge victory in 1964 when the Civil Rights Act was passed. This landmark law banned racial discrimination in restaurants, theaters, motels, hotels, and other everyday gathering spots. It outlawed discrimination by race in public schools, public parks, public libraries, and public pools. It imposed heavy penalties on those who defied the law.

President John F. Kennedy had proposed the legislation

during his time in office, but it was his successor, Lyndon Johnson, who pushed and prodded the bill through Congress. Members of the Southern bloc tried every political trick that they knew to stop the legislation, but their old tactics failed against the new president. Their old alliances with conservative Republicans crumbled.

The Civil Rights Act passed easily: seventy-three senators voted yes, while only twenty-seven voted no, most of them Southerners.

It was a humiliating defeat for Senator Russell, although probably not much of a surprise. President Johnson's political skills were formidable. Everyone in Washington understood this, but no one in Congress appreciated Johnson's talent more than Richard Russell. Over the years, the Georgian had shared everything he knew about power with his colleague from Texas—how to get it, how to use it, and how to keep it.

When Johnson came to the Senate in 1948, after serving more than a decade in the House of Representatives, he wasted no time in endearing himself to Russell. The senator was impressed by the drive and will of Johnson. Perhaps he saw a bit of his younger self in him. Lynda and Luci Johnson, Lyndon's two little girls, grew accustomed to having "Uncle Dick" at family dinners.

Championed by Russell, Johnson rocketed up the ranks of the Senate's Democratic leadership. In 1953, he was chosen as minority leader. Two years later, when his party picked up more seats, he became the Senate's majority leader. In 1956, he flirted with becoming a vice presidential candidate. Four years

The president confers with Senator Richard Russell in the White House, December 7, 1963.

later, he launched a short-lived campaign for the nation's top job.

Like so many gifted students, Johnson eventually outpaced his teacher. He was more personally ambitious than Russell, bolder in his actions, and more ruthless, too. As Russell once explained to a colleague, Lyndon was the sort of man who could twist your arm off at the shoulder, then beat your head in with it.

And there was another important difference: Johnson wasn't a bigot.

When Richard Russell heard the president of the United States promise the American people that "we shall overcome," he knew that the South he had fought so hard to preserve—a place where white people held their advantages over Black people by tradition, by law, or, if it came to it, by violence—

was on its last legs. He understood that once Black Southerners finally went to the polls, they would use their electoral power—the most important power in a democracy—to elect their own candidates and further their own interests.

The generations-long hold that white supremacists like Russell had on the Democratic Party, and much of the United States Congress, was giving way. Shameful excuses for preventing African Americans from voting—the insistence that states' rights were more important than civil rights—were falling on deaf ears.

In a television address watched by millions and applauded by all but a handful of naysayers in Washington, Lyndon Johnson vowed to use the full force of the federal government—its legal as well as its moral authority—to ensure that every American citizen could vote in free and fair elections.

Back home in Georgia, Richard Russell was probably bracing himself. The most powerful man in the world, one of his closest friends, was once again fixing to twist off the Senator's arm, then use the lifeless limb to beat in the ailing man's nearly hairless head.

THE CONFRONTATION OF GOOD AND EVIL
COMPRESSED IN THE TINY COMMUNITY
OF SELMA GENERATED THE MASSIVE
POWER TO TURN THE WHOLE NATION TO
A NEW COURSE.

—MARTIN LUTHER KING JR., MARCH 25, 1965

CHAPTER FIVE

★ ★ ★

SELMA, ALABAMA, MARCH 7, 1965

The Constitution of the United States of America can be read in less than an hour. Some of its passages are confusing, or tricky to interpret, but much of it is clearly and simply written. The Fifteenth Amendment, which was added to the Constitution in 1870, a few years after the end of the Civil War, is especially straightforward:

> The right of citizens of the United States to vote shall not be denied or abridged by the United States or by any State on account of race, color, or previous condition of servitude.
>
> The Congress shall have the power to enforce this article by appropriate legislation.

When it comes to voting, the Fifteenth Amendment promises, your race doesn't matter. The color of your skin doesn't matter. Whether or not you were once enslaved doesn't matter, either. If you are an American citizen and you have been prevented from voting because of your race, your skin color, or because you have been enslaved, you have been wronged. The Constitution, the highest law in the land, is clear on that point.

The amendment also states, just as clearly, that the Congress of the United States has the power to enforce this amendment.

However, for nearly a century, from 1870 until 1965, the Congress of the United States did *not* enforce this section of the Constitution, even though it is just as important as every other section in the Constitution. Every member of the United States Congress, every senator, and every member of the House of Representatives—and every president, too—had pledged an oath "to preserve and protect the Constitution." They promised to honor all of the Constitution, every word of it. Yet for ten decades, the Fifteenth Amendment was openly ignored by many states, especially those represented by Senator Russell and his allies in the Southern bloc.

In the early 1960s, less than one-quarter of the eligible Black voters in the states of the Deep South—Georgia, Alabama, Mississippi, South Carolina, and Louisiana —were registered to vote. In Mississippi, where the population was nearly 50 percent Black, the numbers were especially appalling: a mere 7 percent of its registered voters were African Americans.

Poverty kept many Black people off the voting rolls. So

did physical violence. So did so-called "literacy tests," which required much more than the ability to read. African Americans who attempted to register for their constitutionally mandated right to vote were often given absurdly difficult examinations. They could be asked, for example, to recite an obscure state law, word for word. No mistakes were allowed. Only those with flawless scores on these tests were allowed to register, but there were no flawless scores for Black citizens.

For whites, passing could be as simple as spelling your name properly. Or just getting close to doing so.

Dallas County in Alabama, where the city of Selma is located, had a majority Black population in 1965, but only 1 percent of its registered voters were Black. Schools in the county were segregated by race, even though the Supreme Court of the United States had ruled a full decade earlier, in 1954, that segregated schools violated the Constitution. Public parks in Selma, as well as its restaurants, water fountains, and public restrooms, were segregated by race, despite the recently passed Civil Rights Act of 1964, which expressly prohibited segregation in public places.

Public officials in Selma refused to change their ways just because of criticism from outsiders or decrees from Washington politicians.

Selma was more than just defiant. It was *proudly* defiant.

Jim Clark, the sheriff of Dallas County at the time, decorated his helmet with a Confederate flag decal. He pinned the word NEVER on his lapel. As far as the sheriff of Dallas

County was concerned, nothing was wrong with the way Selma treated its Black citizens, not at all. Selma was *never* going to change. It was doing fine just the way it was.

But when Martin Luther King Jr. and other civil rights leaders looked at Selma, they saw cruelty, hate, and a clear violation of the law. They saw a system of racial inequality that needed to be changed now—not eventually, but right now. They saw an opportunity to shock the conscience of their country.

On December 10, 1964, Dr. King was in Oslo, Norway, receiving the Nobel Peace Prize, "at a moment when twenty-two million Negroes of the United States of America are engaged in a creative battle to end the long night of racial injustice," he said. "I accept this award," he went on, "on behalf of a civil rights movement which is moving with determination and a majestic scorn for risk and danger."

He was at the White House a week later, urging President Johnson to take immediate action on tough new voting rights legislation.

Not yet, said the president. LBJ never enjoyed being told what to do, but he also had practical concerns. A bill still had to be written. Congress still needed to be convinced to pass it. All this took time. There will be a new legislation, he said to Dr. King, soon. Just not right now.

Dr. King chose not to wait. At the start of the new year, the Nobel laureate went to Selma.

The news media followed, as he knew it would.

"Our cry to the state of Alabama is a simple one," King

preached from the pulpit of Brown Chapel on January 2, 1965. "Give us the ballot." More than seven hundred worshippers had crowded into the sanctuary. "We are not on our knees, begging for the ballot," he told the African American congregation. "WE ARE DEMANDING THE BALLOT."

On January 18, Dr. King walked into the Hotel Albert, built by enslaved workers before the Civil War but restricted to white guests ever since, and attempted to register for a room. He was punched in the face by a member of the National States Right Party, a political organization dedicated to the segregation of the races. Then he was kicked in the groin.

The *New York Times* ran a photograph of the assault on its front page.

Four days later, 110 educators, almost the entire membership of the Selma Negro Teachers Association, put on their best clothes and marched to the courthouse, where the voting registration office was located. Sheriff Clark and his deputies greeted them with nightsticks and cattle prods.

On January 25, Dr. King led another march to Selma's courthouse. The marchers were ordered to disperse by Sheriff Clark, and they did disperse, but many insisted upon returning. Tempers flared. One woman who was shoved by the sheriff hit him back hard. The quick-to-anger Clark responded by jumping on her, brandishing his baton.

That altercation was also pictured on the front page of the *New York Times*.

Two hundred sixty-four demonstrators were harassed, then

arrested, on February 1, after still another march to the Dallas County courthouse. Every jail cell in and around Selma was fully occupied. Civil rights protesters grew accustomed to being behind bars, sometimes for a few hours, sometimes for days.

"We're going to turn Selma upside down and inside out," said King, "in order to make it right-side up."

Selma was no longer a small city in the middle of Alabama. It was now the center of the civil rights struggle in America, which meant that it was news, big news. More and more correspondents from major newspapers and magazines, both national and international, found their way to Selma.

Perhaps even more importantly, television crews came, too.

Up in Washington, LBJ was closely monitoring the situation in Alabama. "[A]ll Americans," he said at a press conference on February 4, "should be indignant when one American is denied the right to vote. . . . I intend to see that the right [to vote] is secured for all our citizens."

Privately, Johnson had already ordered his attorney general to make voting rights his top priority. Privately, Johnson had also assured Dr. King that that legislation was coming soon.

But publicly, the president made no promises.

On February 18, five hundred protesters gathered outside the jail in Marion, Alabama, just outside of Dallas County, where the local officials shared Sheriff Clark's contempt for civil rights. The demonstrators had come to Marion to show their support for an incarcerated colleague. The police beat them back with billy clubs and bullets. During the melee, a twenty-

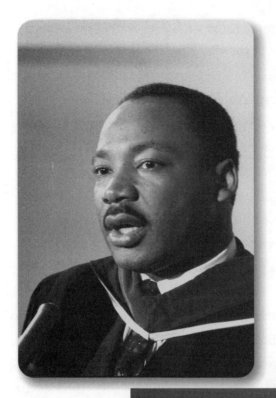

Reverend Martin Luther King Jr. preaches in Selma at the funeral of civil rights worker Jimmie Lee Jackson, March 3, 1965.

six-year-old Baptist deacon, Jimmie Lee Jackson, took two shots in the abdomen as he tried to protect a family member. Eight days later, he died.

Reverend King presided over the deacon's funeral. Members of the news media sat in the pews, faithfully recording every detail of the service.

On the afternoon of Sunday, March 7, a few days after Mr. Jackson was laid to rest, six hundred men and women set out on what they planned would be a fifty-four-mile march from Selma to Montgomery, the capital of Alabama. Unsure whether they would spend the night on the side of the road or in a jail cell, they packed toothbrushes, bedrolls, and other small personal items. They were committed to nonviolent protest. They carried with them no guns, no knives, no weapons of any kind.

Reverend King wasn't at the head of the march that day. He wasn't in Selma. He was several hundred miles away, preaching at his home church in Atlanta. Younger men took the lead. One of them, John Lewis, a son of Alabama sharecroppers who would later become a distinguished congressman, was just a few weeks past his twenty-fifth birthday.

The plan was to walk out of Selma, cross the Alabama River on the Edmund Pettus Bridge, and then continue along US Route 80 to Montgomery.

George Wallace, the staunchly segregationist governor of Alabama, had ordered a hundred state troopers to stand along the far side of the bridge, across the river from Selma. The troopers were outfitted with helmets and equipped with masks to protect themselves from the tear gas they carried. Sheriff Clark's men lined the bridge, several of them astride horses. They came armed with lengths of rubber tubing wrapped in barbed wire.

As the protesters walked across the bridge, the state troopers ordered them to stop and turn around. Unsure of how to respond, the leaders of the march took a moment to pray for guidance. That brief pause, however, turned out to be too long for the patience of the troopers. They charged on the marchers. So did Sheriff Clark's men.

Hundreds of civil rights protesters were beaten, including John Lewis, whose skull was fractured.

Two of the fifteen thousand demonstrators in Harlem on March 15, 1965, a few hours before LBJ addresses Congress.

Five protesters lost consciousness and collapsed on the bridge. Seventy-eight ended up in the hospital.

Later that night, *Judgment at Nuremberg*, an Academy Award–nominated movie about the post–World War II trial of high-ranking Nazis, was making its highly promoted television debut. The network interrupted the film to broadcast a breaking news alert—fifteen minutes of graphic footage that had been shot by television crews that afternoon. Millions of Americans watched with mounting horror as the brutality in Alabama spilled over into their living rooms.

Dr. Martin Luther King rushed back to Selma. Two days later, he stood at the front of yet another march across the Alabama River. Gathered behind him were now over two thousand people, including white ministers who had answered Dr. King's call to come to Alabama. On the far side of the Edmund Pettus Bridge stood five hundred state troopers. As the marchers started to cross the bridge, the officers parted, like a great human gate swinging open.

Dr. King was taken by surprise. He had been promised by state officials, after some quiet negotiations, that the troopers would *block* the marchers, although they would not use any violence this time. In turn, Dr. King agreed that he would direct his marchers to turn around on the bridge, to peacefully return to Selma.

He intended this march to be symbolic. He wanted it to be a display of determination, not another brutal confrontation. Were the state troopers leading his people into a trap on the other side of the river?

Dr. King didn't know—no one knew—so he stopped, prayed, and then retreated. The marchers he led back to Selma were bewildered. None of them had any idea that Dr. King had been talking to state officials. Some of them were furious. Where were the voting rights they were demanding? What was the point of nonviolent resistance if nothing ever changed?

That evening, three white ministers, two from New England and one from California, were set upon by white segregationist thugs. One of them, Reverend James Reeb, from Boston, died from his head injuries two days later.

As the whole world watched with rising dread, the situation in Selma escalated from bad to awful to lethal. What could the federal government of the United States do to stop the bloodshed? What should the president of the United States do?

I DON'T BELIEVE IN LUCK. YOU LOOK INTO IT AND YOU'LL FIND IT'S ALWAYS A LOT MORE THAN JUST LUCK.

—LYNDON JOHNSON, EXPLAINING HOW TO GET AHEAD IN POLITICS

CHAPTER SIX

★ ★ ★

WASHINGTON, DC, DECEMBER 1931

Lyndon Johnson would always be a teller of tall tales, a lover of barbecue, and a wearer of ten-gallon hats. His speech never lost its Texas twang. His gait never dropped its swagger. But when he moved to Washington at the end of 1931, the twenty-two-year-old discovered where he truly belonged.

"You just had to look around," he said, remembering his heady first days in the capital, when it occurred to him that passersby on the street "were probably congressmen at least, maybe senators, members of the cabinet. And there was the *smell* of power. It's got an odor, you know, power, I mean."

Like a bloodhound—or natural-born politician—Johnson had been tracking the scent of power since boyhood, when he slid under the family table to eavesdrop on the governor of

Texas. Briefly, after graduating from San Marcos, he considered making education his career. Employed for a year as debate coach at a Houston high school, he transformed a so-so squad into a powerhouse team that nearly took home the state championship.

But a silver medal wasn't good enough for the rookie educator, and a golden one might not have been good enough, either. Even in his early twenties, the ambitions of Lyndon Johnson were too big to be satisfied by high school competitions.

After Lyndon successfully managed an acquaintance's campaign for the Texas state legislature, his name began to circulate among Lone Star State politicians who were looking for talented aides. Richard Kleberg, who had just won a special election to the United States House of Representatives, offered a job to the young debate coach but gave him almost no time to weigh the pros and cons of the career switch or ponder the challenges of uprooting to a distant city where he knew practically no one. The new congressman needed immediate help in Washington and an immediate answer.

Of course, Lyndon's answer was yes.

As it happened, Congressman Kleberg was an exceptionally lazy man. Heir to the sprawling King Ranch, a South Texas spread that was larger than at least two states, the forty-one-year-old took little interest in legislation and even less in policy. He preferred golf to government, and was easier to find on a fairway than behind his desk on Capitol Hill.

Kleberg's personal shortcomings suited his new hire just fine. Every letter sent to the congressman was first read by his eager assistant. Every letter sent out by the congressman was written by his eager assistant—or by someone hired by Lyndon, supervised by Lyndon, and who could put up with Lyndon hovering nearby, demanding perfect spelling, perfect punctuation, and perfect obedience.

Even the congressman's loving letters to his mother were penned by his aide.

Typically, Lyndon's day started at dawn. By 7:30 a.m., he was at the office. He allowed himself a brief midday lunch, then continued working until around 7 p.m. After dinner, he would either talk politics with his friends, most of them other congressional staffers, or go back to the office for another few hours. Next day, same routine.

The word *workaholic* wouldn't be coined for another twenty years, but it perfectly described Lyndon Johnson. He worked as long as he could. He slept as little as possible. No success was fully satisfying. No achievement was truly enough. He always wanted more.

When Johnson arrived in Washington, President Herbert Hoover occupied the White House, but he wouldn't be there for much longer. Hoover was a brilliant engineer and a distinguished humanitarian, among the most accomplished men of his generation, yet his presidency was a dismal failure. This wasn't entirely his fault. The Iowa-born Republican had the misfortune of taking office just before the Great Depression took hold of America, the greatest economic disaster in the nation's history.

Almost all of Hoover's efforts to ease the suffering of his fellow citizens failed. He had cruised to an easy victory in the 1928 election. Four years later, he was crushed by his Democratic opponent, Franklin Delano Roosevelt.

Voters in 1932 didn't just reject their Republican president, they turned their back on his entire party. Democrats won a huge majority of seats in the House of Representatives. They gained control of the Senate, too.

Roosevelt, whose aristocratic name sounded less imposing when it was whittled down to its initials, FDR, came into office with overwhelming support from ordinary American citizens, but there was nothing the least bit ordinary about the man himself. The former governor of New York, a Harvard graduate who also took classes at Columbia Law School, hailed from a wealthy and prominent family. He was a cousin of Theodore Roosevelt and the husband of the former president's niece.

He was also paralyzed, unable to walk after being stricken with polio in his late thirties. President Roosevelt governed the country from a wheelchair, a fact that was well known at the time by political insiders, but largely hidden from the American public. (Back then, before the internet and cell phone cameras, some secrets were a little easier to keep.)

In his inauguration speech, one of the most famous in American history, Roosevelt offered hope. "The only thing we have to fear," he reassured the nation, "is fear itself."

Immediately after taking office, the new president launched a dizzying number of new federal programs to prop up the cratering economy and restore the confidence of a shaken people. He called this all-out effort the New Deal.

Failing banks were immediately closed and then reorganized by the federal government. Federally funded job programs were created to employ the unemployed. Federally funded

Franklin Delano Roosevelt campaigns for the presidency by car in 1932. Many Americans were unaware that he had been unable to walk for more than a decade.

cash payments were sent to farmers whose crops couldn't find buyers, despite the growing ranks of hungry Americans. Federally funded work began on massive new dams and power projects.

Lyndon Johnson loved the New Deal.

He was the son of Rebekah and Sam Johnson, after

all. The civic-minded Johnsons taught their oldest son that government should be used—maybe even *must* be used, especially in hard times—to lift the lives of everyday people. Government could be a powerful force for good. Lyndon always believed that.

But he also knew that the New Deal offered many exciting opportunities for ambitious young men like himself.

Never shy about pushing his way into closed meetings or private offices, Lyndon made sure the president's top advisors, and eventually the president himself, knew his name, knew about his accomplishments, and knew where his loyalties lay. He made sure that everybody who was anybody in Washington knew that Lyndon Baines Johnson, from the great state of Texas, was all in for the New Deal.

His boss, Congressman Kleberg, however, was not.

Although a member of the Democratic Party—in the 1930s, every congressman and senator from Texas was a Democrat, a situation that would change radically in the decades to come—Kleberg liked nothing at all about the New Deal. He thought President Roosevelt was proposing too much government spending, too much government interference, too much government, period. More often than not, the representative from Texas's Fourteenth District was a reliable vote *against* his fellow Democrat.

Not surprisingly, tension escalated between the hard-driving, Roosevelt-loving Johnson and his work-shy, Roosevelt-hating boss. By the summer of 1935, it was obvious to both men that it was past time for Lyndon to move on from running

Newlyweds Lyndon and Lady Bird in front of the Capitol Building in Washington, DC, soon after their November 1934 wedding in San Antonio.

Kleberg's office on Capitol Hill. So, Lyndon quit (or was fired—no one knew for sure, perhaps not even Lyndon).

Four years toiling as a poorly paid congressional aide was more than long enough. Besides, the twenty-seven-year-old was a married man now, with a young wife to support.

In September of 1934, a mutual friend introduced Lyndon to Claudia Taylor, who acquired the nickname Lady Bird when she was a toddler in East Texas. On their first date, a drive around Austin, he proposed marriage to the shy but enormously smart twenty-one-year-old University of Texas graduate. Lady Bird assumed her talkative companion was kidding, but he wasn't. Less than two months later, most of which the pair spent fifteen hundred miles apart, Lyndon decided he had waited long enough. He and Lady Bird married in a hurried ceremony at a San Antonio church. No family witnessed the event. The bride's mother had died years before, and her father wasn't invited. Neither were her in-laws. The new Mrs. Johnson's wedding ring came from the jewelry counter at Sears. It cost $2.50, which wasn't very much, even then.

Lyndon wasn't unemployed for long. President Roosevelt rewarded his admirer with a big and important job in his home state: director of the Texas branch of the National Youth Administration, the NYA. Johnson was in charge of building, staffing, and administering a brand new program dedicated to boosting the educational and employment prospects of teenagers and young adults throughout the sprawling state. He was twenty-six, only a few years older than many of the young Texans he was aiding.

As always, Lyndon threw himself into the challenge, working nearly nonstop. His wife was expected to feed, water, entertain, and sometimes house the endless stream of coworkers and colleagues that her husband brought to their door, often without any notice.

Their new marriage had already taken on a pattern that would continue throughout their nearly forty years together: he demanded, she delivered.

The job was perfect for Johnson, and he loved it. But at the end of February 1937, after less than two years at the NYA, he resigned, effective immediately.

HE'D COME ON JUST LIKE A TIDAL WAVE SWEEPING ALL OVER THE PLACE. HE WENT THROUGH WALLS. HE'D COME THROUGH A DOOR, AND HE'D TAKE THE WHOLE ROOM OVER. JUST LIKE THAT. EVERYTHING.

—HUBERT HUMPHREY ON SERVING IN THE SENATE WITH LYNDON JOHNSON

CHAPTER SEVEN

★ ★ ★

AUSTIN, TEXAS, FEBRUARY 28, 1937

Everyone who knew Lyndon knew that eventually he was going to run for public office. It was just a matter of time.

On February 28, 1937, his time came.

Congressman James P. Buchanan, a seventy-one-year-old Democrat, had dropped dead of a heart attack six days earlier. For twenty years, Buchanan had represented the Tenth Congressional District of Texas, which included Lyndon's hometown of Johnson City. The veteran legislator left behind a wife and a son and golden ticket for twenty-eight-year-old Lyndon: an open seat in his home district.

Few things are more attractive to an aspiring politician than the chance to run for an open seat, instead of against an incumbent standing for reelection.

Two days after Buchanan's funeral, Johnson quit his job at the National Youth Administration and announced that he was running for Congress. Every second counted. A special election to fill the seat was scheduled for April 10, just five weeks away.

Lyndon turned to his father, the former Texas legislator, for political advice, and to his father-in-law, a rich man, for money. Mr. Taylor, who liked to be called Colonel Taylor despite his lack of military experience, shared almost none of his son-in-law's political beliefs, especially the young man's enthusiasm for the New Deal. But the East Texan couldn't resist his only daughter's request for help, or his son-in-law's drive for success. Taylor contributed ten thousand dollars to Lyndon's campaign, a sizable sum in the late 1930s.

The Tenth Congressional District of Texas covered an enormous area, almost eight thousand square miles. Lyndon campaigned nearly every inch of it. "I support Franklin Roosevelt the full way, all the way, every day," he vowed on his campaign flyers, which he pressed into every hand he could find. His hope was that FDR's enormous popularity in the district would rub off on his faithful acolyte.

Johnson campaigned for the seat as if his life depended it. And in a way, it did—at least, his political life. If Lyndon lost this first race for Congress, who knew when he would have a second chance?

Maybe never.

But Lyndon did win. (Although he lost his appendix on the eve of the election, which meant he savored his victory from a hospital bed while recovering from emergency surgery.) He returned to Washington as an important person, a duly elected congressman, no longer a mere aide. Johnson asked *his* aides to refer to him by his initials, LBJ. Just like FDR.

The young congressman secured a new city hall and fire station for Austin, a new federal building in Elgin, and a new schoolhouse in Johnson City. These were his starter projects. Bigger ones followed. "He wanted water," remembered an aide, "he wanted dams, he wanted all the rural electrification he could get."

LBJ got what he wanted.

"The thing that made Lyndon different from other people," observed a friend from that era, "was that when he started doing something, he poured every ounce of his energy into it. . . . He didn't hold back anything. He just pounded and pounded on it."

By the end of the 1930s, decades after electricity was commonplace for most Americans, ranchers and farmers in the Hill Country could finally flip a switch and light up their homes.

They thanked LBJ for that.

Johnson was unopposed when he ran for reelection in 1938. He ran unopposed in 1940, too. He probably could have spent the rest of his life in the House of Representatives, faithfully serving the people of his district and steadily climbing the leadership ladder in Congress. But that wasn't his idea of success. There were 430 in the House of Representatives at that time. Outside of their districts, almost nobody knew their names.

Representative Johnson wanted to be *Senator* Johnson. He longed to join a smaller, more powerful legislative body, an exclusive club that allowed all its members—if they were bold enough—to become national figures.

In the spring of 1941, nine months before the United States entered World War II, Senator Morris Sheppard, of Morris County, Texas, died of a brain hemorrhage. His sudden demise produced another open seat that the thirty-four-year-old congressman from Johnson City would be more than happy to fill. Lyndon waged a grueling, hard-fought campaign, visiting every corner of his gigantic state.

He came within a whisker of winning.

But he lost. And he lost because his campaign director, twenty-four-year-old John Connally (a future governor of Texas), made a rookie mistake.

After the votes were cast, but before all of them were officially counted, an overly confident Connally bragged to the press about the exact size of Johnson's vote lead. This information made it easy for Johnson's opponent in the race, the sitting governor, Wilbert Lee O'Daniel—or Pappy, as the former flour salesman liked to be called—to conveniently "discover" a forgotten stash of ballots in south Texas, just enough to put him over the top.

Lyndon took the defeat hard. President Roosevelt, who had plenty of experience in the hard-knuckled world of New York state politics, explained a basic fact of electoral life to his heartbroken protégé. "Lyndon," said FDR, "when the election is over, you have to sit on the ballot boxes."

Congressman Johnson was reelected in 1942, when he was on the other side of the globe, serving in the Navy during

A novelty in 1948, LBJ's helicopter attracts crowds and makes it easier for the senatorial candidate to campaign statewide.

World War II. He won again in 1944 and 1946. He became a father for the first time when Lynda Baines Johnson was born in 1944. He became a father for the second time when Luci Baines Johnson arrived in 1947.

He waited, not so patiently, for another shot at a Senate seat.

In 1948, after seven unproductive years in Washington, Pappy O'Daniel lost interest in being a senator, and another open seat finally popped up in Texas. Another bruising campaign ensued. This time, Lyndon won, although just by a whisker.

His margin of victory, in an election in which both Johnson and his opponent, Coke Stevenson, were justifiably accused of voter fraud, was a measly eighty-seven votes.

He acquired a mocking new nickname, Landslide Lyndon.

The new senator shrugged off the teasing—a win is a win, after all—and focused on his new job. His close friendship with Senator Richard Russell paved the way for his rapid rise from rookie senator in 1949, to minority leader in 1953, to majority

The Johnson family in 1948: Lynda (born 1944), Lady Bird, Luci (born 1947), and Lyndon.

leader in 1955, but Lyndon was the engine of his own success. He was brilliant at crafting legislation and even better at building consensus, finding ways to convince other senators—Democrats and Republicans—to vote with him.

In 1957, under Johnson's leadership, and despite the opposition of the Southern bloc, the Senate passed its first civil rights law in nearly a hundred years. Three years later, it passed another. Both pieces of legislation were weak. Segregationists and white supremacists continued to exclude, harass, and disenfranchise Black Americans. But those two pieces of legislation were valuable steps toward a more just America—or so LBJ insisted in later years—and they boosted his national reputation.

LBJ made a brief, lackluster run for the presidency in 1960. A fellow Democratic senator, the telegenic John Fitzgerald

Portrait of the majority leader of the Senate, September 1955. Johnson is elevated from minority leader to majority leader when the Democrats gain seats in the chamber.

Kennedy from Massachusetts, won their party's nomination, then asked Johnson to be his vice presidential running mate. Their Republican opponents were Richard Nixon, the current vice president, and his running mate, Henry Cabot Lodge, who had once been a senator from Massachusetts (until he lost his seat to Kennedy in 1952).

On November 9, 1960, Kennedy was elected president of the United States, and Johnson became vice president. Their margin of victory was tiny, but Johnson was used to that.

VICE PRESIDENT LYNDON JOHNSON HAS LEFT THE HOSPITAL IN DALLAS, BUT WE DO NOT KNOW TO WHERE HE HAS PROCEEDED.

—WALTER CRONKITE, CBS NEWS ANCHOR, NOVEMBER 22, 1963

CHAPTER EIGHT

★ ★ ★

DALLAS, TEXAS, NOVEMBER 22, 1963

Sarah Hughes was in too much of a rush to pick up the judicial robe she kept in her chambers at the federal courthouse in Dallas. She didn't have time to outfit herself in her formal garb to administer the oath of office to Lyndon Johnson, so she presided over the ceremony in a polka-dotted dress.

Like everyone else in the country that day—everyone except, perhaps, for one man—Judge Hughes had no inkling that November 22, 1963, would be an inauguration day. She had plans to attend a political lunch at the Trade Mart in downtown Dallas. Instead, she was rushed a few miles to the northwest, to Love Field, and hustled onto Air Force One.

The presidential aircraft was hot when she came aboard, and getting hotter. Although the engines were on, the air

President Lyndon Baines Johnson is inaugurated in Dallas, aboard Air Force One, on November 22, 1963. Newly widowed Jacqueline Kennedy (right) stands beside him.

conditioning was off, and it would stay off until Air Force One was airborne. The big plane wasn't going anywhere until the swearing-in ceremony was over.

This was by order of the soon-to-be-inaugurated thirty-sixth president of the United States of America.

LBJ was an impatient boy who had grown into an even

more impatient man, but he wasn't just indulging his restless temperament when he ordered Judge Hughes to drop everything and come to Love Field. Yet several people aboard the plane that afternoon, most of them aides who had spent their professional lives alongside the thirty-fifth president of the United States, John F. Kennedy, were appalled by Johnson's insistence on an immediate inauguration.

A slapdash ceremony was undignified, they thought, and disrespectful, too. It wasn't even necessary. When a president dies, the vice president takes over the president's office. That seemed clear from the Constitution and from tradition. Vice President Johnson didn't need an official swearing-in ceremony to become President Johnson.

Why not wait a few hours? Why not allow the plane to return to Washington? Why not give its despairing passengers some time to mourn? Why such god-awful haste at such a god-awful time?

A nation of nearly two hundred million people was heartsick, fearful that more horrors—more assassinations, more confusion, more losses—were still to come.

Lyndon Johnson understood this. He understood this because he, too, was heartsick, and he, too, was scared. He feared for his own life, and for the lives of his wife and their two daughters. He feared for his country.

This was exactly why Johnson acted so quickly. He believed that in these worst of times—maybe especially in these worst of times—the American people needed to know that their country would endure. They needed to see their new commander-in-chief. They needed to know that someone was in charge.

Right here, on Air Force One. Right now, at 2:38 p.m.

More than two dozen men and women, including a carefully positioned photographer and several reporters, shoehorned themselves among the desks and chairs in the plane's stateroom. They watched the tallest man in the room—the tallest man in most rooms he entered—raise his right hand, then place his left on a missal, the prayer book used by Roman Catholics during their celebration of the Mass. It wasn't a Bible—Johnson would use his family Bible at his *second* presidential inauguration, on January 20, 1965—but the volume he touched was sacred, and not strictly because of the prayers it offered the faithful.

This particular missal had belonged to President Kennedy, the first Catholic ever to hold the office.

Almost exactly two hours earlier, President and Mrs. Kennedy had been riding in an open-topped limousine, waving at thousands of supporters who lined the sidewalks of downtown Dallas. Two cars behind the president, Vice President and Mrs. Johnson sat in their own open-topped vehicle, also waving, but few paid them much attention. The throng of onlookers was there for the handsome forty-five-year-old president and his elegant thirty-four-year-old wife.

John Connally, the governor of Texas (and the campaign manager of LBJ's unsuccessful 1941 senatorial campaign), and his wife, Nellie, shared the limousine with the Kennedys.

They sat in front of the presidential couple, perched on jump seats—small foldout seats that faced forward. Mrs. Connally was buoyed by the size of the crowd, and probably a little relieved, too.

President and Mrs. Kennedy in their motorcade through downtown Dallas on November 22, 1963, accompanied by Texas governor John Connally and his wife, Nellie.

Earlier that morning, a full-page ad in a major Dallas newspaper—paid for by a committee of self-proclaimed "free-thinking and American-thinking citizens"—had scornfully questioned the patriotism of Kennedy and other top members of his administration. Dark rumors were swirling around town that the president's safety could be in jeopardy during his visit.

Mrs. Connally leaned back toward John Kennedy and encouraged him to enjoy the affection of her state's second-largest city.

"You certainly can't say that Dallas doesn't love you," she told him.

When the tip of a rifle peeked out of a third-floor window of the Texas School Book Depository building, those on the ground who saw it believed the weapon was there for the president's protection. The eyewitnesses assumed it belonged to a Secret Service agent, a state policeman, or maybe a local officer, but it didn't. They were all wrong about the intentions of the man holding the firearm that afternoon.

Even now, decades after the tragedy, no one really knows for sure why Lee Harvey Oswald did what he did, but at 12:30 p.m., the twenty-four-year-old father of two, a recently hired worker at the warehouse, aimed his deadly weapon, pulled its trigger, and fired.

The president and the governor were both hit. Their limousine sped to the nearest hospital, Parkland Memorial, where the two men were raced into surgery. Governor Connally's wounds were serious, but not fatal. He lived for nearly thirty more years.

President Kennedy's wounds were mortal. Jacqueline Kennedy believed that her husband died in the car, in her arms. The doctors at Parkland officially pronounced him dead at 1 p.m.

While Lyndon Johnson took his presidential oath of office, the body of John Kennedy lay at the rear of Air Force One. Mrs. Kennedy, who had stepped away from her husband's casket, stood beside the new president of the United States as he vowed to preserve, protect, and defend the Constitution.

John Kennedy had made those same promises to the American people on a frigid January day in 1961. His wife was radiant in her pale, fur-trimmed coat. Her brimless hat inspired millions of American women to toss out their old headgear and put on the sleek new style.

But now, less than three years later, no one wanted to copy the outfit that Mrs. Kennedy wore to the inauguration of her husband's successor: a blood-streaked pink suit, tattered stockings.

A few moments before the ceremony, in an effort to be helpful, Mrs. Johnson had reminded Mrs. Kennedy that fresh clothes were available in the well-stocked closets of Air Force One. The thoughtful fifty-year-old was sure that her younger friend, always so careful about her appearance, would want to step out of her ruined garments before she appeared before the cameras.

No, said Jacqueline Kennedy. No, she did not.

"I want them to see," she explained, "what they have *done* to Jack."

In that sad, crowded, overheated stateroom on Air Force One, at a ceremony that ended almost as soon as it began, the grief-stricken widow and the incoming president stood at each other's side. But they were sending two very different signals to the American people.

Lyndon Johnson wanted to reassure his country that its democratic institutions were strong and steady. The United States had withstood the traumas of a civil war. It had survived a crushing Great Depression. It had prevailed over fascism during World War II.

An assassin's bullet, no matter how cruel, would not destroy America.

Mrs. Kennedy, on the other hand, was determined to show the nation just how much it had lost.

On one of the worst days in American history, one of the darkest days in his own life, Lyndon Baines Johnson became president of the United States. Step by methodical step—as a congressional aide, member of the House of Representatives, senator, and vice president—he had made himself into one of the most accomplished elected officials of his time, or any time. As he ascended the political ladder, the fifty-five-year-old always had his eye on the presidency.

But Johnson never wanted to get to the Oval Office this way. Not because of a gun, especially not one that was fired in Texas.

A little more than two hours after departing from Dallas, the presidential plane landed at Andrews Air Force Base, outside of Washington. While the casket bearing his predecessor was lowered from the cargo hold and loaded into an ambulance, Johnson waited inside the aircraft. While Mrs. Kennedy, still in her bloodied clothes, took her place beside her late husband, he waited. While the ambulance drove away, bound for the Bethesda Naval Hospital, where John Kennedy's body would be autopsied and prepared for burial, he waited.

Then Lyndon Baines Johnson walked out of Air Force One, stood before the whirring cameras and the tangle of microphones, and made his first official statement to the American people as their duly inaugurated president.

"I will do my best," he promised a shattered nation. "That is all I can do."

SOUTHERNERS PLAYED A MOST
MAGNIFICENT PART IN ERECTING THIS
GREAT DIVINELY INSPIRED SYSTEM OF
FREEDOM, AND AS GOD IS OUR WITNESS,
SOUTHERNERS WILL SAVE IT.

—GOVERNOR GEORGE WALLACE,
INAUGURATION SPEECH, MONTGOMERY,
ALABAMA, 1963

CHAPTER NINE

★ ★ ★

THE WHITE HOUSE, WASHINGTON, DC, MARCH 13, 1965

L yndon Johnson was a man of faith, although you wouldn't know it from his behavior. His cursing would make a sailor blush; his lies were as countless as the stars in the West Texas sky. Over his decades of marriage to Lady Bird, he twisted his wedding vows beyond recognition. He loved money and power, and didn't fret much about how he acquired either. Only a major heart attack in 1957, an event that nearly killed him, halted his chain-smoking and hard drinking. Even so, eventually, LBJ returned to both vices.

Yet despite all of his failings, or maybe because of them, President Johnson was a devout Christian with an abiding belief in the goodness of people. The great-grandson of George Washington Baines, a Baptist minister who became the president of Baylor University, and the son of Rebekah Baines Johnson, a pious graduate of her grandfather's university, Lyndon Baines Johnson knew his Bible inside and out, Old and New Testaments.

At the beginning of difficult negotiations, he regularly recited his favorite verse from the Book of Isaiah: "Come now, let us reason together, saith the Lord." In the Old Testament, it's followed by this passage: "Though your sins are like scarlet, they shall be as white as snow."

What Isaiah promised—and what Johnson truly believed— was that every person, even those who have committed great sins, *can* change for the good. All of us can *be* better. All of us can *do* better.

Even Lyndon Baines Johnson. Even in his fifties.

Throughout his political career, LBJ's primary focus had been on himself and on power. For decades, he did not speak out against the civil rights abuses that were widespread in Texas and throughout the South. He did not push to desegregate schools that kept Black children and white children in separate and completely unequal classrooms. He did not fight for the right of Black Americans to share the same restaurants, hotels, and restrooms as white Americans. He settled too often for face-saving gestures and easy-to-break promises of racial equality.

As he made his way up to the Oval Office, Johnson was careful not to alienate white colleagues, powerful leaders like Senator Richard Russell, who believed in white supremacy. He tried not to agitate white voters in Texas, many of whom were suspicious of the civil rights movement and distrustful of its leaders.

But when John Kennedy died in 1963, Lyndon Johnson became the president of every state in the union, not just the states of the Old Confederacy. He answered to every American, those who supported him and those who didn't. In one horrifying instant, he achieved his lifelong dream: he became the most powerful person in the most powerful nation in the world. The weight of his new responsibilities was enormous, perhaps even overwhelming. Every bit of himself was required to get the job done: intelligence, cunning, relentlessness, determination, and wit. He was especially shameless about exploiting his intimidating size.

But he also drew upon a less obvious facet of his character: his faith in the deep-seated decency of people, including people who had done truly horrible things.

As tensions rose in Alabama and calls grew for federal action, perhaps even military action, LBJ encouraged his aides to show compassion for their fellow Americans. "Most Southern people don't like this violence," he told staff members, many of whom had grown up well north of the Mason-Dixon Line. "They know deep in their hearts that things are going to change. They may not like it, but they will accommodate."

When President Johnson took the measure of Alabama's governor, George Wallace, he found in him a quality that almost no one else saw in the race-baiting, hate-mongering, attention-seeking politician. The charismatic Alabaman had barreled onto the national stage in 1963, when he stood on the steps of the

Alabama governor George Wallace speaks at the Democratic National Convention in Atlantic City, New Jersey, August 1964.

capitol in Montgomery during his gubernatorial inauguration and made this vow to a cheering crowd of white supporters: "Segregation now, segregation tomorrow, segregation forever." Two years later, on Bloody Sunday, Wallace expressed no remorse when his state troopers beat up hundreds of peaceful marchers in Selma.

But Johnson believed that Wallace understood, deep in his heart, that change was inevitable, that a new era of civil rights was dawning in the Deep South, that the old system of denying Black Americans their constitutional right to vote was dead wrong.

LBJ suspected that George Wallace wasn't really all that different from himself. He had a hunch that Governor Wallace was capable of shame.

Wallace invited himself to the White House on March 13, 1965, a few days after Bloody Sunday and a few days before Johnson's voting rights speech. This was a remarkably nervy move. Few governors, or any other sort of public official, would have had the gall to push their way into the Oval Office. But even though Johnson was normally thin-skinned about slights to his presidential authority, he raised no objection when Wallace announced that he was coming to the White House to discuss ways to prevent further violence.

The president said he would be delighted to speak with his fellow Democrat.

This should have worried Wallace, but it didn't. Accustomed to getting his way back home, Wallace was confident he could hold his own during a private conference with the president. He hadn't heard Richard Russell's warnings about how expertly Lyndon Johnson could dismember an adversary.

When George Wallace walked into the Oval Office, he couldn't have anticipated that he was about to be held captive, more or less, for three and a half hours. He couldn't foresee that this meeting would turn out to be one of the longest three and a half hours of his life.

Slight in build, almost a foot shorter than the president,

Governor Wallace (in doorway, second from left) tries to block Black students from enrolling at the University of Alabama, June 11, 1963.

Wallace was seated on a white couch, plushly upholstered with cushions that were so deep and so soft that they could almost swallow whole an unwary occupant. Positioning himself directly across from the governor, in a rocking chair that was in nearly constant motion, LBJ swung into his steadily declining visitor, sometimes getting so close that the two men—one huge and leaning in, the other small and sinking down—were practically nostril to nostril.

Protesters were outside the Oval Office that day—protesters of all sorts regularly stationed themselves outside the White House during the Johnson years, a situation that the Texan accepted as constitutionally protected but personally annoying.

"George," said the president, directing his visitor's attention to the clatter on the street, "wouldn't it be just wonderful if

Civil rights activists demonstrate near the White House, March 12, 1965.

we could put an end to all those demonstrations?"

Wallace was quick to agree. No one supported "law and order"—a popular slogan for the principle that citizens must always obey the law and public officials must always maintain order in their districts—more eagerly than the governor.

"Well," suggested Johnson, perhaps during an extra-close swing in the vicinity of the governor's nose, "why don't you and I go out there . . . and let's announce that you've decided to" let the Blacks in your state vote?

No, that's impossible, the governor replied. He didn't have the power, he argued, to single-handedly change the voting laws in Alabama. In his home state, local officials were in charge of voter registration, not state officials. As governor of Alabama, he was duty bound to honor state law. Regrettably, he simply didn't have the legal authority to do what Johnson wanted.

Balderdash, LBJ shot back, although he used a different word. Stop lying to me, he thundered. Stop fooling around with the president of the United States. Those weren't his exact words, either.

"George," LBJ said, shifting his tone and softening his language while continuing to rachet up the pressure, "why are you doing this? You came into office as a liberal. You've spent all your life trying to do things for the poor."

You should be helping all the people of Alabama, not just cheering on its bigots, LBJ scolded. When you're dead and gone, how do you want to be remembered? What do you want etched on your tombstone?

"Do you want a great big marble monument that reads, 'George Wallace—He Built'?" the president asked. "Or do you want a little piece of pine board lying across that harsh caliche soil that reads, 'George Wallace—He Hated'?"

Besieged by the hundreds of reporters and photographers who had been waiting for the meeting to end, the governor of Alabama was uncommonly subdued when he was finally allowed to depart the Oval Office. Normally a man of many words, he could summon only a few to describe his encounter with Johnson. He meekly told the media that the conversation was "frank and friendly." He noted "the courtesy of the president. "

Wallace didn't mention Johnson's explosive bursts of profanity. He didn't complain about being physically intim-

The president gestures from his rocking chair in the Oval Office on April 6, 1965, three weeks after Governor Wallace invited himself to the White House.

idated by a man with the oversized proportions of LBJ. He didn't reveal that even the president's couch seemed to be out to get him.

Thoroughly outmatched and totally wrung dry, the governor of Alabama returned home as quickly as he could. He continued to deliver defiant speeches to fired-up. all-white audiences. But he quietly allowed federal officials to come into his state to act as peacekeepers when, on March 21, demonstrators from Selma once again headed for Montgomery.

Four days and fifty-four miles later, the much-delayed march culminated in a rally outside the Alabama State Capitol, the very spot where Wallace had vowed an eternity of racial segregation. The triumphant crowd—some world famous, but

Marchers on their way from Selma to Montgomery, Alabama, March 1965.

most of them everyday American citizens, Black and white, Southerners and Northerners—sang songs about freedom, recited prayers of unity, and pledged their commitment to equal justice for all.

"They told us we wouldn't get here. And there were those who said we would get here only over their dead bodies," Dr. King said, "but all the world today knows that we are here and we are standing before the forces of power in the state of Alabama, saying, 'We ain't goin' to let nobody turn us around.'"

George Wallace didn't venture out of the capitol building during the rally. He worked at his desk, consulted with aides, and kept mostly out of sight. But every now and again, he was spotted standing by himself in front of a window, looking out at the tens of thousands of voting-rights supporters who had come at last to Montgomery.

Years later, making a joke that was more notable for its truthfulness than its humanity, Wallace recalled what it was like to go up against Johnson in the Oval Office. "Hell," he said, "if I'd stayed in there much longer, he'd have had me coming out for civil rights."

But nearly two decades after his afternoon with Johnson—after three more unsuccessful runs for the presidency and a failed assassination attempt in 1972 that kept him in a wheelchair for the last twenty-six years of his life—George Wallace *did* come out for civil rights. Setting himself apart from almost every other major segregationist leader of his era, he asked to be forgiven by the voters of Alabama, especially the Black voters. When he made his final run for governor, in 1982, he was supported by 90 percent of Black voters in his state, making him the only Alabaman in history to serve four terms in the governor's office.

Lyndon Johnson didn't live long enough to witness Wallace's public change of heart. Chances are, he wouldn't have been surprised by it.

NO VOTING QUALIFICATION OR
PREREQUISITE TO VOTING, OR
STANDARD, PRACTICE, OR PROCEDURE
SHALL BE IMPOSED OR APPLIED BY ANY
STATE OR POLITICAL SUBDIVISION TO
DENY OR ABRIDGE THE RIGHT OF ANY
CITIZEN OF THE UNITED STATES TO VOTE
ON ACCOUNT OF RACE OR COLOR.

–FROM SECTION 2 OF
THE 1965 VOTING RIGHTS ACT

CHAPTER TEN

★ ★ ★

WASHINGTON, DC, AUGUST 6, 1965

Governor George Wallace didn't fly to Washington to witness the signing of the Voting Rights Act. Senator Richard Russell from Georgia skipped the ceremony, too. Very few elected officials from the South were in the rotunda of the United States Capitol that afternoon.

But Martin Luther King Jr. sat in a place of honor. So did Roy Wilkins, head of the NAACP, the National Association for the Advancement of Colored People. So did Rosa Parks, who, a decade earlier, had launched the Birmingham, Alabama, bus strike that forced the desegregation of the city's public transportation system.

John Lewis, recovered from the head wounds he suffered in Selma, was there.

Civil rights leaders and activists crowded into the great round room on August 6, 1965. They came to celebrate their

After signing the Voting Rights Act on August 6, 1965, LBJ congratulates Martin Luther King Jr.

enormous victory. They came to rejoice.

The Voting Rights Act had sailed through Congress. In the House of Representatives, 328 members voted for the law. Only seventy-four voted against it. The margin of success in the Senate was equally lopsided: seventy-nine yeses to nineteen nos.

The Southern bloc had been thoroughly humiliated.

President Johnson spoke from a podium emblazed with the presidential seal. "Three and a half centuries ago, the first Negroes arrived in Jamestown," he said, referring to 1619, when enslaved Africans were first brought to England's colony in Virginia. "They did not arrive in brave ships in search of a home for freedom. They didn't mingle fear and joy, in expectation that in this New World anything would be possible to a man strong enough to reach for it. They came in darkness and they came in chains."

The dignitaries gathered in the rotunda weren't the audience that LBJ was speaking to that day. Ordinary American citizens, especially white American citizens, who were watching on televisions or listening to radios or reading newspapers—these were the millions that President Johnson wanted to influence. His speech was intended for Americans who had never been denied their right to vote or participated in a civil rights march or spent a terrifying night in a small-town jail. His words, he hoped, would eventually reach the children of those Americans, not just their current crop of kids, but their grandchildren and great-grandchildren and on through the generations.

Johnson wanted his speech to reach *you*.

At long last, the president said, after more than three hundred years, the shameful split in the American experience— a straight path to liberty for white people and a tortured one for Black people—would be mended at the voting booth. The Voting Rights Act, which he was just about to sign into law, ensured that all Americans, regardless of the color of their skin or the location of their home, could fully participate in their own governing. They could vote.

"[T]he heart of the act," the president said, "is plain."

But the new law had more than just a good heart. It also had very sharp teeth.

Any attempt to evade the Voting Rights Act, to undermine its clear and specific requirements, would be met with a

The array of pens used on July 10, 1965, for the signing of the Housing and Urban Development Act.

harsh and immediate response from the federal government. The president announced that the state of Mississippi, which required its voters to pay a poll tax—a fee for voting—would be sued by the United States within the next twenty-four hours.

Officials from the Department of Justice, the agency of the federal government that oversees enforcement of the laws enacted by Congress, would immediately begin to draw up a list of states, or localities within states, that were in clear violation of the new law. Federal workers would start registering voters in those locations. Lawsuits would shortly be filed against three more states that charged poll taxes: Alabama, Virginia, and the president's home state, Texas.

Any individual who willfully violated the Voting Rights

Act could be fined up to five thousand dollars and sentenced to up to five years in prison.

"I pledge you," the president vowed, "that we will not delay, or we will not hesitate, or we will not turn aside until Americans of every race and color and origin in this country have the same right as all others to share in the process of democracy."

His remarks over, Johnson walked down a familiar corridor to the Senate's side of the Capitol, where dozens of VIPs squeezed into the ornately decorated chamber known as the President's Room. They clustered around a small, simple desk—the same desk that Senator Johnson had used when he served as Senate majority leader. They applauded as President Johnson signed his name to the Voting Rights Act, officially making it the law of the land.

Less than two years after his hurried presidential inauguration at Love Field, Johnson had grown accustomed to signing landmark pieces of legislation. He had become expert at making the most of the moment, changing writing instruments with each twist and curl in his name, rewarding supporters with a barely used pen as a souvenir of the occasion.

On April 9, 1965, in tiny Stonewall, Texas, seated at a wooden table in front of the one-roomed Junction School, beside his first teacher, Miss Kate (now Mrs. Loney), President Johnson signed the Elementary and Secondary School Act.

Outside his first school, beside his first teacher, LBJ signs the Elementary and Secondary Education Act, April 11, 1965.

The new law transformed the role of the federal government in local schools, greatly expanding funding and raising academic standards.

On July 30, 1965, in Independence, Missouri, the hometown of former president Harry Truman, LBJ signed the legislation that established Medicare and Medicaid. The two programs provided health care and insurance to older Americans and lower-income Americans. Eighty-one-year-old Truman, who proposed similar legislation during his administration a quarter century earlier, was handed the first-ever Medicare card.

On Liberty Island for the signing of the Immigration Act, October 3, 1965.

More signing ceremonies were to come that year. Many more. A groundbreaking immigration bill was swiftly moving through Congress. So was legislation to combat water pollution; legislation to aid colleges and universities; legislation to establish a National Endowment for the Arts, which supported cultural programs; and legislation to create the Department of Housing and Urban Development, a cabinet-level department primarily focused on improving life in America's cities.

Johnson had been reelected in a landslide on November 3, 1964. He bested his Republican opponent, Senator Barry

PUBLIC LAW 89-*170*

S. 1564

Eighty-ninth Congress of the United States of America

AT THE FIRST SESSION

Begun and held at the City of Washington on Monday, the fourth day of January, one thousand nine hundred and sixty-five

An Act

To enforce the fifteenth amendment to the Constitution of the United States, and for other purposes.

Be it enacted by the Senate and House of Representatives of the United States of America in Congress assembled, That this Act shall be known as the "Voting Rights Act of 1965".

SEC. 2. No voting qualification or prerequisite to voting, or standard, practice, or procedure shall be imposed or applied by any State or political subdivision to deny or abridge the right of any citizen of the United States to vote on account of race or color.

SEC. 3. (a) Whenever the Attorney General institutes a proceeding under any statute to enforce the guarantees of the fifteenth amendment in any State or political subdivision the court shall authorize the appointment of Federal examiners by the United States Civil Service Commission in accordance with section 6 to serve for such period of time and for such political subdivisions as the court shall determine is appropriate to enforce the guarantees of the fifteenth amendment (1) as part of any interlocutory order if the court determines that the appointment of such examiners is necessary to enforce such guarantees or (2) as part of any final judgment if the court finds that violations of the fifteenth amendment justifying equitable relief have occurred in such State or subdivision: *Provided,* That the court need not authorize the appointment of examiners if any incidents of denial or abridgement of the right to vote on account of race or color (1) have been few in number and have been promptly and effectively corrected by State or local action, (2) the continuing effect of such incidents has been eliminated, and (3) there is no reasonable probability of their recurrence in the future.

(b) If in a proceeding instituted by the Attorney General under any statute to enforce the guarantees of the fifteenth amendment in any State or political subdivision the court finds that a test or device has been used for the purpose or with the effect of denying or abridging the right of any citizen of the United States to vote on account of race or color, it shall suspend the use of tests and devices in such State or political subdivisions as the court shall determine is appropriate and for such period as it deems necessary.

(c) If in any proceeding instituted by the Attorney General under any statute to enforce the guarantees of the fifteenth amendment in any State or political subdivision the court finds that violations of the fifteenth amendment justifying equitable relief have occurred within the territory of such State or political subdivision, the court, in addition to such relief as it may grant, shall retain jurisdiction for such period as it may deem appropriate and during such period no voting qualification or prerequisite to voting, or standard, practice, or procedure with respect to voting different from that in force or effect at the time the proceeding was commenced shall be enforced unless and until the court finds that such qualification, prerequisite, standard, practice, or procedure does not have the purpose and will not have the effect of denying or abridging the right to vote on account of race or color: *Provided,* That such qualification, prerequisite, standard, practice, or procedure may be enforced if the qualification, prerequisite, standard, practice, or procedure has been submitted by the chief legal officer or other appropriate official of such State or subdivision to the Attorney General and the Attorney General has not interposed an objection within sixty days after such

The first and last pages of the Voting Rights Act, with the president's signature.

S. 1564—10

Sec. 17. Nothing in this Act shall be construed to deny, impair, or otherwise adversely affect the right to vote of any person registered to vote under the law of any State or political subdivision.

Sec. 18. There are hereby authorized to be appropriated such sums as are necessary to carry out the provisions of this Act.

Sec. 19. If any provision of this Act or the application thereof to any person or circumstances is held invalid, the remainder of the Act and the application of the provision to other persons not similarly situated or to other circumstances shall not be affected thereby.

Speaker of the House of Representatives.

Vice President of the United States and
President of the Senate.

APPROVED

AUG - 6 1965

Goldwater from Arizona, by an astounding sixteen million votes. His political coattails—his ability to sweep other Democrats into office—were long. Democrats won two-thirds of the seats in the House of Representatives and increased their majority in the Senate.

Not every Democrat in Congress agreed with the president's ambitious agenda—Southern Democrats usually did not—but LBJ could count on a deep base of support within his own party, and he knew how to win over Republican legislators, too.

No other president, not even Franklin Delano Roosevelt, had been able to pass so much major legislation in such a short amount of time. No other president had extended the reach of the federal government into so many corners of everyday life: school rooms, hospitals, homes, polling booths, and courthouses, and into the water Americans drink and the air they breathe.

"In a land of great wealth," Lyndon Johnson said on January 20, 1965, at his second inauguration, "families must not live in hopeless poverty."

This inauguration was filled with pomp and pageantry, witnessed by more than a million well-wishers in Washington and tens of millions from their homes. The Chief Justice of the Supreme Court wore his black robe when he administered the oath of office to Johnson. He didn't have to hurry to get himself to the ceremony.

"In a land rich in harvest," the president declared, "children just must not go hungry. In a land of healing miracles, neighbors must not suffer and die untended. In a great land of

learning and scholars, young people must be taught to read and write."

The six-foot, three-inch president leans into Supreme Court justice Abe Fortas, July 1965.

Back in the 1930s, President Roosevelt used a three-word phrase—The New Deal—to describe his multifaceted program to lift a struggling nation out of the Great Depression. Thirty years later, his protégé from Texas found his own three-word slogan—The Great Society—to describe his plan to extend the prosperity of a great nation to all Americans, regardless of their race or their age or their wealth or their country of origin.

The president in the Oval
Office, January 24, 1966.

He wanted to build this Great Society as soon as possible. Maybe even sooner than possible. Patience was never among LBJ's strengths.

"Don't waste a second," Johnson implored his staff at the beginning of 1965, driving them as relentlessly as he drove himself. "Get going *right now*."

Time would always be Johnson's greatest enemy. There was never enough time for him to do everything he wanted to do.

There was never enough time for him to achieve everything he wanted to achieve. Every ambitious person feels this way, perhaps ambitious politicians feel this even more deeply, but Johnson's race against time was especially intense.

And it was doomed.

"Every day that I'm in office and every day that I push my program," Johnson explained to his staff just days after his second inauguration, "I'll be losing part of my ability to be influential because that's in the nature of what a president does."

"Something is going to come up," LBJ predicted, "either something like the Vietnam War, or something else, where I will begin to lose all that I have now."

Time proved him to be dead right about that.

I HAVE LIVED—DAILY AND NIGHTLY—WITH THE COST OF THIS WAR. I KNOW THE PAIN THAT IT HAS INFLICTED. I KNOW, PERHAPS BETTER THAN ANYONE, THE MISGIVINGS THAT IT HAS AROUSED.

—PRESIDENT LYNDON JOHNSON,
MARCH 31, 1968

CHAPTER ELEVEN

★ ★ ★

VIETNAM AND WASHINGTON, 1955–1968

Disasters come in a variety of speeds. Some strike quickly: hurricanes, earthquakes, and tornados wreak their destruction in a matter of hours or minutes, sometimes even seconds. Others take their time, like the droughts that turned the farmlands of the Hill Country into dust, or wars that grind on year after year, disrupting millions of lives, killing millions of people.

The Vietnam War was a slow-moving sort of disaster. It began in 1955, before Johnson became president, and it lasted until 1975, long after he left the Oval Office. But Vietnam would always be known as LBJ's disaster, and he always knew that he would be blamed for the catastrophe.

Trouble was, he didn't know how to stop it.

Instead, he just made it worse.

Around sixteen thousand American military personnel

The commander-in-chief observes flight exercises above Fort Campbell, Kentucky, July 23, 1966.

were stationed in South Vietnam when President Kennedy was assassinated in November 1963. Located in Southeast Asia, along the South China Sea, South Vietnam had been formally established as a nation less than a decade earlier, but it already had a long, complicated, and bloody history. All of Vietnam, both its northern and southern portions, had been controlled by France for nearly a century. Japan occupied the land during World War II, from 1940 until the war ended in 1945. Then the French reasserted their claim on Vietnam, sparking a seven-year conflict, sometimes known as the First Indochina War, which ended when French forces were decisively defeated by Vietnamese fighters in the Battle of Dien Bien Phu.

In 1954, in an attempt to make peace in a region long

battered by warfare, diplomats from seven nations gathered in Geneva, Switzerland. They agreed to temporarily divide Vietnam into two countries: North Vietnam and South Vietnam. An invisible line on the globe, the seventeenth parallel, separated the two nations.

South Vietnam was supposed to be a free and democratic country where citizens had a voice in their own governing, respected a set body of laws, and voted in fair elections. But it wasn't a democratic country—not really. Its elections were neither free nor fair; winners were decided long before the first vote was ever cast. The leaders of South Vietnam, with few exceptions, were both incompetent and appallingly corrupt. Their top priority was enriching themselves and their families, not building a democracy.

North Vietnam was a communist country. China, its powerful neighbor to the north, was also a communist country. So was the massive Soviet Union, which stretched all the way from eastern Europe to Asia's Pacific coast. In communist countries, the economy was controlled by the state. The educational system was controlled by the state. The military was controlled by the state.

Private property was strictly limited in communist countries. There was no freedom of speech. There were almost no individual freedoms of any sort.

The communist leaders of North Vietnam may have signed the 1954 agreement that divided their homeland, but they were determined to reunify Vietnam under one rule—*their* rule. North Vietnamese fighters routinely broke into South

Vietnamese territory, breaching the border at the seventeenth parallel, openly defying the Geneva agreement.

The northerners crossing into the south weren't generally seen as invaders. They weren't perceived as foreigners. Many of them were former neighbors and old friends, separated cousins or reunited brothers or long-lost uncles.

President Johnson's predecessors in the White House— Dwight Eisenhower in the 1950s, John Kennedy in the early 1960s—had sent financial aid and military assistance to South Vietnam. They were not, for the most part, motivated by compassion for the suffering people of South Vietnam. Nor did they have much faith in the leadership of the country. But they chose to prop up South Vietnam because they feared what might happen throughout Asia—and eventually, perhaps, inside the United States—if the country failed.

Most American politicians of the era—and most American voters—believed that communist countries posed a mortal threat to democratic societies like the United States. They were convinced that communists, especially those in the Soviet Union, were determined to take over the world, one country at a time.

They believed in the domino theory.

The domino theory explained—or at least, tried to explain—why communism must always be stopped. The theory was hard to prove, but easy to grasp. Imagine a long line of dominoes, each standing a short distance from each other. Now imagine that each of those dominoes is a free and democratic nation.

Tip over the first domino, and all the others tumble. Once one country falls to communism, its neighbors fall, too.

"If you start running from communists," said LBJ to National Security Advisor McGeorge Bundy in May 1964, "they may just chase you right into your own kitchen."

"Yeah, that's the trouble," agreed Bundy, an aristocratic New Englander who held that the United States should never show weakness, especially against communists. "And that is what the rest of that half of the world is going to think if this thing comes apart on us. That's the dilemma."

"It's just the biggest damn mess that I ever saw," Johnson complained. "I don't think it's worth fighting for, and I don't think we can get out."

In a nutshell, this was his worry: if America didn't send more American troops into South Vietnam, then South Vietnam would be taken over by North Vietnam.

A few months later, while campaigning for reelection in the fall of 1964, Johnson downplayed the escalating conflict on the other side of the world. "We are not," he vowed, "about to send American boys nine or ten thousand miles from home to do what Asian boys ought to be doing for themselves."

Yet he *was* sending American boys to Vietnam—and American girls, too, most of them serving in medical capacities—and he was also sending American tanks, planes, and warships into the region. By the end of 1964, there were 23,000 American soldiers in Vietnam. By the end of 1965, the number had ballooned to more than 184,000.

In the summer of 1965, attempting to justify why he was

shipping even more troops to Vietnam, Johnson made an appeal to the conscience of his fellow Americans: "We did not choose to be the guardians at the gate, but there is no one else."

Did the Vietnamese people *need* a guardian? Did they even *want* a guardian? In a war where civilians and combatants were hard to differentiate, American bombs were flattening South Vietnamese villages, American chemicals were poisoning South Vietnamese fields, American soldiers were shooting South Vietnamese children. Was living in a communist society really worse than being saved by the American military?

Who, exactly, were Americans helping? The suffering people of South Vietnam or the failing government of South Vietnam?

In his State of the Union address in January 1966, Johnson declared, "I believe that we can continue the Great Society while we fight in Vietnam." Vowing to build upon his earlier legislation, he pressed for new programs that would boost employment in struggling neighborhoods, impose safety standards for cars, strengthen the enforcement of civil rights laws, and protect rivers and streams from pollutants.

But Johnson's influence over Congress was waning, just as he predicted it would. His job approval rating among the American people was slipping, too.

His new social programs were expensive and complicated to administer. Civic unrest was rising. In the summer of 1965, thirty-four people died in Watts, a primarily African American neighborhood in Los Angeles, when a dispute between police officers and residents erupted into six days of violence.

And his war in Vietnam dragged on.

By the end of 1966, nearly 400,000 American troops were in Southeast Asia. A year later, that number was closer to 500,000.

President and Mrs. Johnson visit wounded soldiers at the National Naval Medical Center in Bethesda, Maryland, October 21, 1965.

Almost 20,000 Americans had died in Vietnam. More than ten times that number of South Vietnamese were gone, too.

Directly across the street from the White House, within earshot of the president and his family, a steady chorus of protesters took turns taunting the most powerful man in the nation. "Hey, hey, LBJ," they chanted from Lafayette Park, "How many boys have you killed today?"

In April of 1967, less than two years after he stood behind Johnson at the signing of the Voting Rights Act, Martin Luther King Jr. used the pulpit of New York City's Riverside Cathedral

Tens of thousands of antiwar protesters come to Washington to march on the Pentagon, October 21, 1967.

to declare his opposition to the war. "Surely this madness must cease. We must stop now. I speak as a child of God and brother to the suffering poor of Vietnam," he said. "I speak for the poor of America who are paying the double price of smashed hopes at home, and dealt death and corruption in Vietnam."

Tens of thousands of antiwar protesters rallied in front of Washington's Lincoln Memorial in October of 1967, and

Martin Luther King Jr. with LBJ in the Cabinet Room of the White House, March 18, 1966.

thousands more continued on to the steps of the Pentagon, the five-sided nerve center of the American military establishment. In more and more homes throughout the country, kitchen walls were adorned with a poster featuring a childlike drawing of a flower and a sobering observation: "War Is not Healthy for Children and Other Living Things."

Every night, when Americans turned on their televisions, gruesome scenes of war filled their screens.

And still, the bloodshed continued. The fighting intensified. In late January of 1968, the North Vietnamese launched

News anchor Walter Cronkite conducts an interview from Vietnam. The war is on the other side of the world, but television newscasts bring it into American living rooms every evening.

a deadly new assault on South Vietnam during the Tet holiday, the Vietnamese New Year. The United States Embassy in Saigon, the capital of South Vietnam, was attacked. So was the presidential palace. So were major military bases and dozens of other targets throughout the country.

The American guardians seemed to have lost control of the gate. Maybe they had never had control of it in the first place.

Nineteen sixty-eight was a presidential election year, the tenth since Johnson first came to Washington as a young congressional aide. Most political observers assumed he would run for reelection, although LBJ hadn't announced his candidacy and his name wasn't printed on the ballot

in New Hampshire, which hosted the nation's first presidential primary. Supporters had to write in his name. Senator Eugene McCarthy,

LBJ listens to a tape-recorded message from his son-in-law, Charles Robb, a Marine captain serving in Vietnam, July 31, 1968.

however, had made his own presidential intentions clear. An outspoken critic of the war, the Minnesota Democrat inspired legions of college-aged supporters to zip up their parkas, pull on their snow boots, and trudge door to

President Johnson announces from the Oval Office that he will not run for another term, March 31, 1968.

door in a frigid New England winter. When New Hampshire's votes were tallied on March 12, McCarthy stunned the nation by coming within a few percentage points of defeating a sitting president.

A little more than two weeks later, on March 31, 1968, Johnson addressed the American people from his desk in the Oval Office. Although not yet sixty, he looked much older on that Sunday evening. The burdens of his job had left their mark. Worry lines scored his forehead, deep creases gouged his cheeks. For nearly forty minutes, the president spoke about the war in Vietnam and urged all Americans to come together and join him in the pursuit of a lasting peace in Southeast Asia.

This vital work, he declared, must be pursued without political considerations or partisan causes.

"Accordingly," he said, "I shall not seek, and I will not accept, the nomination of my party for another term as your president."

And then, for the first time that evening—or for maybe much longer—LBJ looked happy.

LYNDON, I'M GOING BACK TO THAT
LITTLE HOUSE IN THE HILLS WHERE
PEOPLE KNOW WHEN YOU'RE SICK AND
CARE WHEN YOU DIE.

—LYNDON JOHNSON, REMEMBERING HIS
FATHER'S LAST REQUEST

CHAPTER TWELVE

★ ★ ★

AUSTIN, TEXAS, DECEMBER 12, 1972

Ignoring the advice of his doctor, who feared that the former president's heart was too weak for the trip, and weather forecasters, who warned that the icy roads might do him in even faster, Lyndon Johnson traveled sixty treacherous miles from his home in Stonewall, Texas, to his presidential library in Austin on December 12, 1972.

Since departing the White House nearly four years earlier, LBJ had mostly stayed out of the spotlight. He tended his ranch, spoiled his grandchildren, and established his library and a school of public affairs at the University of Texas. He also produced, with the assistance of some long-suffering ghostwriters, a dull and dignified memoir: *The Vantage Point: Perspectives on the Presidency, 1963–1969*. Not surprisingly, almost no one read it.

Threats to life and limb weren't enough to keep the sixty-

The sixty-four-year-old former president at his ranch in Stonewall, Texas.

four-year-old at home, not when so many distinguished civil rights leaders had come to Texas for a two-day civil rights symposium at the Johnson Library. Among the event's honored guests: eighty-one-year-old Earl Warren, who served as chief justice of the Supreme Court when it ruled in *Brown v. Board of Education* that racial segregation was unconstitutional; sixty-six-year-old Thurgood Marshall, who argued the winning side of that 1954 case and was now, having been appointed by Johnson, the first African American to serve on the Supreme Court; and thirty-six-year-old Barbara Jordan, the first African American woman to be elected to the House of Representatives from the state of Texas.

Every seat in the library's ample auditorium was occupied by scholars, students, activists, or old friends of Lyndon and

Lady Bird. Standees crowded along the back wall and spilled out into the corridor.

A view of Johnson's archives from the great hall of his presidential library in Austin, Texas.

Johnson took his time getting up to the stage when his moment came to speak. He used both hands to steady himself at the podium. He pulled a nitroglycerin pill out of his pants pocket a few minutes into his remarks, then slipped the heart medication into his mouth as unobtrusively as possible.

You didn't need a medical degree to see that the former president's body was failing. Many in the auditorium must have feared that they were witnessing Johnson's last public appearance, and they were right to worry. A little more than a month later, alone in his bedroom at the ranch, he would suffer a massive heart attack and die.

But LBJ's health wasn't his audience's only cause for concern on that wintery day. The future of his Great Society programs was in jeopardy as well.

President Richard Nixon, a Republican critic of many of Johnson's policies, had just been reelected by a huge margin, even greater than LBJ's 1964 landslide victory. With the exception of Massachusetts and the District of Columbia (not a state, but represented in the Electoral College), every state in the nation voted for Nixon on November 7, 1972. Once again, the Old Confederacy voted as a solid bloc, but it was no longer a Democratic bloc. Most white Southern voters, devoted Democrats since the Civil War, now backed the Republican president, a lukewarm supporter of civil rights legislation.

In Vietnam, the war raged on. Nixon assured Americans in 1968 that he had a secret plan to end the war. He was lying, as it turned out, but that campaign promise may have helped him eke out a narrow victory over Hubert Humphrey, Johnson's vice president. Four years later, when Nixon was reelected, far fewer American soldiers were on the ground in Southeast Asia, although the war was far from over.

(The conflict didn't end until 1975, when the North Vietnamese finally succeeded in reuniting all of Vietnam under communist rule. By then, Nixon was no longer president. A political scandal known as Watergate had forced him to resign a year earlier.)

Racial tensions in America hadn't been lessened by the passage of the Civil Rights Act and the Voting Rights Act. In fact, they appeared to be increasing.

The assassination of Martin Luther King Jr. in April 1968, gunned down by a white supremacist, sparked a series of anguished uprisings in more than a hundred cities, including Chicago, Detroit, Newark, and Baltimore. In Washington, DC, the threat to the security of the national government appeared to be so great that armed Marines stood guard on the steps of the Capitol Building. After Dr. King's death, a new generation of Black

After the assassination of Martin Luther King Jr., major cities throughout America erupt in deadly rioting. Armed military personnel stand guard over the Capitol Building, April 8, 1968.

leaders rose to prominence; many of them questioned the late reverend's dedication to nonviolence and urged confrontation. Middle-class white Americans continued to move away from racially mixed urban centers and into racially segregated suburbs.

And another Kennedy was dead. Two months after Dr. King's assassination, Senator Robert Kennedy, the younger brother of the late president, was shot to death on the night he won the 1968 California presidential primary.

Everyone who came to hear LBJ speak on December 12, 1972, even the youngest students, knew how tumultuous the last few years had been for the United States. Everyone in the auditorium that day understood how divided the American people had become.

But LBJ hadn't come to Austin to dwell on disappointments.

He had come to Austin to do what he had done throughout his political career: to push, to prod, to urge others to work longer, smarter, and aim higher. He came to inspire a new crop of public servants, to support their commitment to justice and reinforce their dedication to the nation's founding principles of equality. He came to remind his audience, as the prophet Isaiah counseled in the Old Testament, that great things happen when people reason together.

Johnson had been racing against the clock for his entire life. Now that he had so little time left, he wasn't going to waste it.

"I believe," he said, "that the essence of government lies with unceasing concern for the welfare and dignity and

decency and innate integrity of life for every individual."

Then he added, just to be sure there was no misunderstanding his intentions, "I don't like to say this, and I wish I didn't have to add these words to make it clear, but I will: regardless of color, creed, ancestry, sex, or age."

Barbara Jordan, the first Black woman from the South to be elected to Congress; Vernon Jordan (no relation), president of the National Urban League; and LBJ at his last public appearance, December 12, 1972.

Much had been achieved in civil rights during the last ten years, he acknowledged. The old Jim Crow laws were gone. The restrictions against Black voters were gone. Throughout the South, thanks to the Voting Rights Act, the number of African American voters was soaring.

Johnson praised the contributions of several members of his audience, but he wasn't satisfied.

"I don't want this symposium to come here and spend two days talking about what we have done. The progress has been much too small. We haven't done nearly enough. I'm kind of ashamed of myself that I had six years and couldn't do more than I did. I'm sure all of you feel the same way about it."

Johnson wanted more. He always wanted more.

"We know there is discrimination and hate and suspicion, and we know there is division among us."

Deep-seated prejudices die hard. Old bigotries can outfox new laws.

"But there is a larger truth," he insisted. "We have proved that great progress is possible. We know how much still remains to be done."

Eight years earlier, in the best speech of his life, President Johnson came to the great hall of the House of Representatives to assure the country that he stood with those who were fighting for the rights of all American citizens to fully participate in their own democracy. At the close of the last speech of his life, in a library that preserved the full record of his long career—proof of his great successes, and evidence of his deepest failures—he made his final appeal to a great nation.

"And if our efforts continue, and if our will is strong, and if our hearts are right, and if courage remains our constant companion, then, my fellow Americans . . ."

He leaned over the podium and lifted his voice.

"I am confident," he said, "that we shall overcome."

EPILOGUE

★ ★ ★

SUPREME COURT OF THE UNITED STATES, 2013

A lot can change over the course of half a century.

When Lyndon Johnson became president in 1963, there were five African Americans in the House of Representatives. None were Southerners. No African Americans sat in the Senate.

In 2013, forty-five African Americans served in the House. Nineteen of them hailed from the states of the Old Confederacy. There were three Black senators, including Tim Scott, a Republican from South Carolina.

A Black man, Barack Obama, was in his second term as president of the United States. In 2008, he beat John McCain, a war hero and senator from Arizona. Four years later, he bested Mitt Romney, a successful business leader and popular governor from Massachusetts.

In 2012, for the first time in history, Black citizens went to the polls at a higher rate than white: 66 percent of eligible African Americans voted in the presidential election, which was two percentage points more than white voters.

"I am where I am today," President Obama wrote in a letter to the *New York Times*, "only because [voting rights activists] refused to accept anything less than a full measure of equality."

The Voting Rights Act was able to reach middle age because of broad support from both chambers of Congress. In the decades that followed its initial passage, the law was revised, enlarged, and renewed on four different occasions, and each time was approved by larger margins. Its 2006 renewal sailed through the Senate without a single dissenting vote.

But the law still had powerful detractors. It was faulted for being unduly harsh on Southern states. It was characterized as a prime example of the federal government seizing too much power for itself. In the twenty-first century, a new generation of critics relied upon several arguments to challenge the legality of the legislation, but at the heart of their complaints was a simple idea:

The Voting Rights Act wasn't necessary anymore. The era of widespread racial discrimination at the voting booth had ended.

In 2013, in a case known as *Shelby County v. Holder*, the Supreme Court agreed, but only by the slimmest of margins, five justices to four. "History did not end in 1965," Chief Justice John Roberts declared in the opinion he wrote for the majority. "Our country has changed, and while any racial discrimination in voting is too much, Congress must ensure that the legislation it passes to remedy that problem speaks to current conditions."

Although the entire Voting Rights Act wasn't overturned, the Supreme Court pulled out some of its sharpest teeth. A key provision—a set of standards that determined whether a state or locality had a malicious history of racial discrimination at the polls—was deemed unconstitutional. As a result, jurisdictions whose voting laws had previously been strictly monitored by the federal government—a process known as "preclearance" required the Department of Justice to approve all changes— now had a much freer hand to set their own policies.

The practical effects of the ruling were felt almost immediately. Several state legislatures, especially in the South, rewrote their election laws, requiring specific sorts of identification from voters, pruning tens of thousands of registered voters from the voting rolls, and limiting early voting opportunities. These new laws were enacted swiftly. Preclearance was no longer necessary.

State lawmakers insisted that they were simply trying to prevent voter fraud, but these tighter restrictions on voters were challenged in the courts as being just a way to keep racial minorities from the polls. In Washington, congressional supporters of the Voting Rights Act struggled to find a way to replace the provision that the Supreme Court invalidated.

After the *Shelby County v. Holder* ruling, the future of one the greatest achievements of President Johnson's Great Society was uncertain.

But then again, the future of the Voting Rights Act had always been uncertain.

Back in 1963, when he first proposed the law, President Johnson was clear-eyed about the challenges it faced. "Many of the issues of civil rights are very complex and most difficult," he admitted to Congress. "[E]ven if we pass this bill, the battle will not be over."

Some fights must be fought again and again. Some values must be defended over and over.

"But about this there can be and should be no argument," the president insisted. "Every American citizen must have an equal right to vote. There is no reason which can excuse the denial of that right. There is no duty which weighs more heavily on us than the duty we have to ensure that right."

★ *TIMELINE* ★

1941-1942	Serves on active duty in US Navy during World War II
NOVEMBER 2, 1948	Elected to Senate
JANUARY 3, 1953	Becomes minority leader of Senate
JULY 20, 1954	Vietnam divided into North Vietnam and South Vietnam
JANUARY 4, 1955	LBJ becomes majority leader of Senate
NOVEMBER 8, 1960	Elected vice president of the United States
NOVEMBER 22, 1963	President Kennedy assassinated; President Johnson inaugurated on Air Force One
JUNE 2, 1964	Civil Rights Act signed by LBJ
NOVEMBER 3, 1964	Wins landslide electoral victory in presidential election
JANUARY 2, 1965	Martin Luther King Jr. arrives in Selma, Alabama
MARCH 7, 1965	"Bloody Sunday" march in Selma, Alabama
MARCH 15, 1965	LBJ introduces Voting Rights Act
AUGUST 6, 1965	Signs Voting Rights Act
DECEMBER 1966	385,000 American troops in Vietnam
OCTOBER 21, 1967	50,000 antiwar protesters march in Washington
JANUARY 30, 1968	North Vietnamese begin Tet Offensive
MARCH 31, 1968	LBJ announces he won't run for reelection
APRIL 4, 1968	Martin Luther King Jr. assassinated
NOVEMBER 5, 1968	Richard Nixon elected president
JANUARY 20, 1969	Nixon inaugurated; LBJ retires to ranch in Stonewall, Texas
JANUARY 22, 1973	Dies at ranch

★ ACKNOWLEDGMENTS ★

I want to thank Paul Harrison, senior faculty member of the Middlesex School, for reading an early version of this book and then nudging me to do better. I also want to thank David Kolker of the Campaign Legal Center for deftly explaining election law to a civilian. And I'm eternally grateful to Robert Carey, who introduced me to Paul and David, and so much else.

★ NOTES ★

Chapter One: Washington, DC, March 15, 1965

x   **"It is wrong—deadly wrong":** Lyndon Johnson, special message to Congress: "The American Promise," March 15, 1965 (LBJ Presidential Library). All quoted passages in this chapter are from the same speech.

Chapter Two: Stonewall, Texas, August 27, 1908

8   **"Didn't matter where he was, he was always running, running, running":** Jessie Johnson Hatcher, remembering her nephew's childhood. Merle Miller, *Lyndon: An Oral Biography* (New York: G. P. Putnam's Sons, 1980), 16.

12   **"He's a chip off the old block":** Eddie Hahn to Sam Johnson. Miller, 8.

18   **"Sitting there in the half-light of dawn":** Lyndon Johnson remembering his childhood. Robert Caro, *The Years of Lyndon Johnson: The Path to Power* (New York: Knopf, 1982), 104.

19   **"If you want a business to be jinxed":** Tom Johnson on Lyndon's father. Caro, *Path to Power*, 85.

21   **"My children were born to lead":** Rebekah Johnson on her family. Caro, *Path to Power*, 95.

21   **"That boy is going to wind up":** Ruth Baines on her grandson. Caro, *Path to Power*, 102.

Chapter Three: Cotulla, Texas, 1927

22   **"I was determined to give them":** Lyndon Johnson on his students in Cotulla, Texas. Doris Kearns Goodwin, *Lyndon Johnson and the American Dream* (New York: Harper & Row, 1976), 66.

28   **"Great as an educator":** Lyndon Johnson on the president of his college. Caro, *Path to Power*, 149.

29   **"I've just met a boy":** Professor David Votaw to a colleague. Caro, *Path to Power*, 143.

29   **"He was never popular":** College classmate Willard Deason. Miller, 30.

31   **"He was the kind of teacher":** Manuel Sanchez, Cotulla student. Caro, *Path to Power*, 169.

32   **"I was determined to spark something":** Lyndon Johnson on his students in Cotulla. Goodwin, 66.

Chapter Four: Winder, Georgia, March 15, 1965

34   **"I am in favor of giving both the whites and the blacks":** Senator Richard Russell. Caro, *The Years of Lyndon Johnson: Master of the Senate* (New York: Knopf, 2002), 194.

38   **"Any Southern white man worth a pinch of salt":** Senator Richard Russell. Caro, *Master of the Senate*, 191.

38   **"the welfare and progress of both races":** Senator Richard Russell. Caro, *Master of the Senate*, 183.

38   **"The whites and blacks alike in our section":** Senator Richard Russell. Caro, *Master of the Senate*, 183.

39   **"I was brought up with them":** Senator Richard Russell. Caro, *Master of the Senate*, 182.

42   **"We've had our problems":** Senator Richard Russell. Caro, *Master of the Senate*, 197.

Chapter Five: Selma, Alabama, March 7, 1965

46   **"The confrontation of good and evil":** Martin Luther King. "Our God Is Marching On" speech, March 25, 1965 (Martin Luther King Jr. Research and Education Institute, Stanford University).

50   **"at a moment when twenty-two million Negroes":** Martin Luther King. Nobel Peace Prize acceptance speech, December 10, 1964 (King Institute, Stanford University).

50   **"Our cry to the state of Alabama":** Martin Luther King. Nick Kotz, *Judgement Days: Lyndon Baines Johnson, Martin Luther King, and the Laws that Changed America* (Boston: Houghton Mifflin, 2005), 254.

52   **"We're going to turn Selma upside down":** Martin Luther King. Kotz, 264.

52   **"[A]ll Americans should be indignant":** Lyndon Johnson. Kotz, 267.

Chapter Six: Washington, DC, December 1931
58   **"I don't believe in luck":** Lyndon Johnson. Miller, 40.
59   **"You just had to look around":** Lyndon Johnson. Miller, 38.
62   **"The only thing we have to fear":** Franklin Roosevelt, inaugural address, 1932 (Franklin Delano Roosevelt Presidential Library and Museum).

Chapter Seven: Austin, Texas, February 28, 1937
68   **"He'd come on just like a tidal wave":** Hubert Humphrey on Senator Johnson. Miller, 175.
71   **"He wanted water":** James Rowe Jr. on Lyndon Johnson. Miller, 69.
71   **"The thing that made Lyndon different from other people":** Virginia Foster Durr. Miller, 69.
72   **"Lyndon, when the election":** Franklin Delano Roosevelt. Miller, 88.

Chapter Eight: Dallas, Texas, November 22, 1963
76   **"Vice President Lyndon Johnson has left the hospital":** CBS News bulletin, November 22, 1963.
82   **"You certainly can't say that Dallas":** Nellie Connally to President Kennedy. Caro, *The Years of Lyndon Johnson: The Passage to Power* (New York: Knopf, 2012), 311.
83   **"I want them to see":** Jackie Kennedy to Lady Bird Johnson. Caro, *The Passage to Power*, 330.
85   **"I will do my best":** Lyndon Johnson. Caro, *The Passage to Power*, 365.

Chapter Nine: The White House, Washington, DC, March 13, 1965
86   **"Southerners played a most magnificent part":** George Wallace, inaugural address, January 14, 1963 (Alabama Department of Archives and History).
89   **"They know deep in their hearts":** Lyndon Johnson to staff. Kotz, 303.
90   **"Segregation now":** George Wallace, inaugural address.
92   **"George, wouldn't it be just wonderful":** Lyndon Johnson to George Wallace. Gary May, *Bending Towards Justice: The Voting Rights Act and the Transformation of American Democracy* (New York: Basic Books, 2013), 113.

94 **"Do you want a great big marble monument":** Lyndon Johnson to George Wallace. May, 114.

96 **"They told us we wouldn't get here":** Martin Luther King, address at the conclusion of the march from Selma to Montgomery, March 25, 1965 (King Institute, Stanford University).

97 **"Hell, if I'd stayed":** George Wallace. Kotz, 306.

Chapter Ten: Washington, DC, August 6, 1965

100 **"Three and a half centuries ago":** Lyndon Johnson, remarks on the signing of the Voting Rights Act (University of Virginia, Miller Center).

108 **"In a land of great wealth":** Lyndon Johnson, inaugural address, 1965 (University of Virginia, Miller Center).

110 **"Don't waste a second":** Lyndon Johnson to staff. Miller, 407.

Chapter Eleven: Vietnam and Washington, 1955–1968

112 **"I have lived—daily and nightly—with the cost of this war":** Lyndon Johnson, remarks on his decision not to seek reelection (Miller Center, University of Virginia).

117 **"It's just the biggest damn mess that I ever saw":** Lyndon Johnson to McGeorge Bundy (Digital History, University of Houston).

117 **"We are not about to send American boys":** Lyndon Johnson, remarks in Memorial Hall, Akron University, October 21, 1964 (Presidency Project, University of California, Santa Barbara).

120 **"Surely this madness must cease":** Martin Luther King, "Beyond Vietnam" speech, April 4, 1967 (King Institute, Stanford University).

125 **"Accordingly, I shall not":** Lyndon Johnson, remarks on his decision not to seek reelection (Miller Center, University of Virginia).

Chapter Twelve: Austin, Texas, December 12, 1972

126 **"Lyndon, I'm going back to that little house":** Lyndon Johnson recalling his father's wish. Goodwin, 89.

132 **"I believe that the essence of government":** Lyndon Johnson, December 12, 1972 (LBJ Presidential Library video). All subsequent quoted passages in this chapter are from the same speech.

★ SELECTED BIBLIOGRAPHY ★

Here are some of the books I relied upon for *Larger Than Life*. All of them are excellent, but the extraordinary work of Robert Caro is in a class of its own. For more than forty years, Mr. Caro has been researching and writing about Lyndon Johnson. Four volumes have already been published. A fifth is coming. I can't wait.

Caro, Robert A. *The Years of Lyndon Johnson: The Path to Power*. New York: Knopf, 1982.

———. *The Years of Lyndon Johnson: Means of Ascent*. New York: Knopf, 1990.

———. *The Years of Lyndon Johnson: Master of the Senate*. New York: Knopf, 2002.

———. *The Years of Lyndon Johnson: The Passage to Power*. New York: Knopf, 2012.

Caroli, Betty Boyd. *Lady Bird and Lyndon: The Hidden Story of a Marriage that Made a President*. New York: Simon & Schuster, 2016.

Goldman, Eric F. *The Tragedy of Lyndon Johnson.* New York: Knopf, 1969.

Goodwin, Doris Kearns. *Lyndon Johnson and the American Dream.* New York: Harper & Row, 1976.

Kotz, Nick. *Judgment Days: Lyndon Baines Johnson, Martin Luther King Jr., and the Laws that Changed America.* Boston: Houghton Mifflin, 2005.

Manchester, William. *Death of a President: November 1963.* New York: Harper & Row, 1967.

May, Gary. *Bending Toward Justice: The Voting Rights Act and the Transformation of American Democracy.* New York: Basic Books, 2013.

Miller, Merle. *Lyndon: An Oral Biography.* New York: G. P. Putnam's Sons, 1980.

Ward, Geoffrey C., and Ken Burns. *The Vietnam War: An Intimate History.* New York: Knopf, 2017.

Woods, Randall B. *LBJ: Architect of American Ambition.* New York: Free Press, 2006.

Online Resources

LBJ Presidential Library

Stanford University: Martin Luther King Jr. Research and Education Institute

University of Virginia: Miller Center

★ *PICTURE CREDITS* ★

63   Franklin Delano Roosevelt Presidential Library and Museum photo by Unknown

65   LBJ Library photo by Unknown

73   LBJ Library photo by Unknown

74   LBJ Library photo by Unknown

75   Library of Congress. Photography by Thomas J. O'Halloran.

78   LBJ Library photo by Cecil Stoughton

81   Photography by Victor Hugo King

90   Library of Congress. Photography by Warren K. Leffler.

92   Library of Congress. Photography by Warren K. Leffler.

93   Library of Congress. Photography by Warren K. Leffler.

95   LBJ Library photo by Yoichi Okamoto

96   Library of Congress. Photography by Peter Pettus.

100   LBJ Library photo by Yoichi Okamoto

102   LBJ Library photo by Yoichi Okamoto

104   LBJ Library photo by Yoichi Okamoto

105   LBJ Library photo by Yoichi Okamoto

106   National Archives and Records Administration

107   National Archives and Records Administration

109   LBJ Library photo by Yoichi Okamoto

110   LBJ Library photo by Yoichi Okamoto

114   LBJ Library photo by Yoichi Okamoto

119   LBJ Library photo by Yoichi Okamoto

120   Library of Congress. Photography by Warren K. Leffler.

121   LBJ Library photo by Yoichi Okamoto

122   National Archives (127-N-A371381)

123   LBJ Library photo by Jack Kightlinger

124   LBJ Library photo by Yoichi Okamoto

128   LBJ Library photo by Frank Wolfe

129   LBJ Library photo by Charles Bogel

131   Library of Congress. Photography by Warren K. Leffler.

133   LBJ Library photo by Frank Wolfe

★ INDEX ★

Note: Page numbers in *italics* refer to illustrations.